CAROLINA SUNRISE

THOMAS TISDALE

UNITED WRITERS PRESS
ASHEVILLE, N.C.

Carolina Sunrise
by Thomas Tisdale

ISBN: 978-1-945338-16-8

Library of Congress Control Number: 2016956649

Second Printing

Cover photograph courtesy of Gaya Mitra

Published by:

United Writers Press
Asheville, N.C. 28803
www.UnitedWritersPress.com

DEDICATION

to
Frederick Cornell Jenkins
a gentle man of Charleston

TABLE OF CONTENTS

Disclaimer

Details and circumstances described in all of the stories included herein are true. However, to preserve the privacy of characters and their families, many of the names of the individuals involved, except in historical references, have been changed.

PREFACE

The Carolina Lowcountry is a narrow sliver of land lying against the Atlantic Ocean on the southeast coast of North America running the length of South Carolina. A rich and vibrant culture has grown up in the more than 300 years since Europeans and their African slaves colonized the land.

The character of the place has sprung from the confluence of cultures that have inhabited it through many generations since the arrival of the first permanent European settlers. The nature of the land: the soil and what grows in the soil, the birds that fly in the air, the fish that swim in the waters, and the mammals, especially the humans, that walk on the surface of the land have molded the richness of the ecosystem of the Lowcountry.

The history of events establishes the setting for all that has happened to make the place what it is, but the antiseptic facts fall short and do not themselves reveal the character of the civilization that was born there nor does it describe the rich patina that has grown and matured on everything that exists. The words of the standard history texts do not reveal the pungent smell of the air from the salt marshes that hover on the coastal plain; nor do they reveal the bright shafts of light from the Carolina moon against the night sky; or the whip of the alligator's tail as it thrashes around in the old rice field canal; or the white wings of the eagle soaring in the air; or the loud rush of noise from the rising covey of quail in a pine forest. Nor do they reveal the hopes, fears, and passions of the men and women who have lived and died there across the centuries. But the history is important to the stories about what really happened because it tells where the people came from and why; it lays the foundation for what is important to future generations of Lowcountry dwellers, but it is merely a foundation. The history of the European and African immigration and the colonial settlements exposes the rich diversity of humanity that first settled the Lowcountry. What springs from the foundation is only a part of the story for the real story lies in the hearts and minds of those who have been born, lived, and died on the land.

The past, like a fast running stream, continually rolls into the present, and into the future, and since the beginning of recorded time, has become intertwined in the affairs of people. The past is present in every human experience. But our senses confine and limit us to experiencing only three dimensions when there is much more. An interesting concept of time in human history has been espoused by several southern writers. The concept is that everything that has happened in a place on earth, in this case, the Carolina Lowcountry, is still present but cannot be consciously seen or experienced by men and women because of the limitations that creation and evolution have imposed on the human sense of dimensions. Some believe there are more than three, but we humans lack the capacity to connect with them.

William Faulkner famously said, "The past is not dead, it's not even past." Andrew Nelson Lytle, another notable southern writer, warns, "if we dismiss the past as dead and not as a country of the living which our eyes are unable to see...then we are likely to become servile...Living as we will be in a lesser sense of ourselves, lacking that fuller knowledge which only the living past can give." And then, T. S. Eliot, in the opening lines of his poem *Burnt Norton* observes,

> "Time present and time past
> Are both perhaps present in time future,
> And time future contained in time past..."

Faulkner, in his Nobel Prize acceptance speech in 1950, said "it is [the writer's] privilege to help man endure by lifting his heart, by reminding him of the courage and honor and hope and pride and compassion and pity and sacrifice which have been the glory of his past. The [writer's] voice need not merely be the record of man, it can be one of the props, the pillars to help him endure and prevail." So too the stories in this book are meant to be a prop to uphold future earth dwellers in the quest to understand life and with it to live more abundantly.

The English were the first to establish a lasting colony in 1670 at a place already inhabited by those we now call Native Americans, but to the English they were Indians because of the mistaken belief that they were on the sub-continent of India. The English colony was organized by influential men who obtained a charter from the monarch to develop Carolina as a commercial venture. They were

17th-century entrepreneurs motivated by the prospect of making money on the venture after several failed earlier attempts. The British colonial system provided a stable base for the growth of Carolina, and would eventually become the United States of America. The colony's promoters, the Lords Proprietors, recruited English farmers on the island of Barbados to spearhead the development. Some of the first settlers brought African slaves with them to provide a source of labor used to grow crops. A need for more laborers for what became a lucrative rice culture led to the development of the slave trade between the New World and Africa that endured for more than a century in North and South America. A great irony of Lowcountry history is that the institution of slavery that the early English settlers introduced, which they in their time believed was morally acceptable, spawned the rich African culture that has shaped the wholeness of life in important ways, and has added great substance to the ethos that exists in the Lowcountry in the 21st century. There have been four waves of French immigration to the Carolina Lowcountry over a period of several centuries beginning in 1670. The first was the 16th-century explorers that settled a place called Charlesfort in Beaufort County. The second came hard on the heels of the arrival of the English from Barbados and their slaves. They were French Protestants called Huguenots, most of whom had earlier left France for England, Switzerland, and other European countries to avoid repression at home before and after the Revocation of the Edict of Nantes in 1685. They were recruited where they had been transplanted, mostly in England and Switzerland, by the colonial organizers to add to the bulk of the developing colony's population. The Huguenots became Charleston merchants, and the farmers among them settled land outside the central town that anchored the colony. The third wave of Frenchmen came midway through the 18th century when the English decided to "resettle" a group of French people living in Nova Scotia. The effect of this resettlement project on Lowcountry life turned out to be temporary as most of the Acadians, as they were called, soon departed leaving no evidence of their presence on the developing civilization.

The fourth wave of French immigrants to the Lowcountry came in 1793 when many French Catholics were forced to leave Haiti in the wake of a rebellion by slaves and former slaves. The 500 or so mostly aristocratic Frenchmen who ended up in Carolina in 1793 brought a strong breath of fresh air to Charleston that was then a little worn down at the heels after more than a century and a quarter of colonial life. This last large influx of Frenchmen contributed a welcomed new luster to the patina of the Lowcountry, which had been dulled by the passage of time since its settlement in 1670.

Several groups of immigrating Irishmen have made valuable contributions to the richness of Lowcountry life beginning in the early days of the Carolina colony. Those first Irish immigrants were mostly English people whose families had settled on Irish estates as a part of the English domination of the land of Ireland. They were mostly Protestants. The English governors of the Carolina colony prohibited the immigration of Roman Catholics to the colony, and there were no significant numbers of them settling in the Lowcountry until after the creation of the United States.

Some of those early English Irishmen became leaders of the colony and of the new nation that took root as the United States grew into nationhood. The Rutledge family exemplifies this group of settlers. Andrew Rutledge, the father of Edward who was a signer of the Declaration of Independence was one of them. Edward's brother, John, was a principal drafter of the United States Constitution and was appointed Chief Justice of the United States by President Washington. A third brother, Hugh, was a prominent South Carolina jurist. Pierce Butler, born in Ireland, was a member of a prominent Lowcountry family, and an early member of the United States Senate from South Carolina.

Another large group of Irish immigrants were the Scots-Irish. They were mostly Presbyterians whose families migrated from Scotland to Northern Ireland and then to America, many of them settling in the Carolina colonies. But most of them settled in the Backcountry, as the land inland from the coastal plain was called. Some of them came to the Lowcountry and added to the rich fabric of coastal life. The Scots Irish immigration to the region continued through the 19th century.

The backbone of Irish immigration to Carolina and to the rest of the country began in about 1815 when massive numbers of them, almost all Catholics, began to arrive. The Roman Catholic Church sent Bishop John England to Charleston, the city that was the focal point of Irish immigration in the South. He formalized the structure of the Church in the southeastern part of the United States. Many more came when the potato famine struck Ireland in 1845. After 1815, many Irish immigrants provided much-needed labor for construction projects across South Carolina. They made an important contribution by building the railroad systems across the State. The Irish workers in the Lowcountry were, as they were generally across the nation, a small but important segment of the overall population.

There were immigrants from many other nations to the Carolina

Lowcountry, but by the early 19th century, the patterns of life had been set by the English, the French, and the Irish, and perhaps most importantly, by the African slaves. They were later joined by the Germans. And Jews came to the Lowcountry from many places including many from the countries of Eastern Europe. In later years, there were Chinese, Vietnamese, Spanish and many from several Latin American countries.

The 20th-century South Carolina leaders of the South Carolina government thought that continued immigration was so important to its growth that early in the century the General Assembly of South Carolina created its own Department of Immigration. Their plan was to aggressively encourage the immigration of new settlers to be brought by ship to the port of Charleston and scattered across the State from the Lowcountry to the Piedmont to replace the slave labor that evaporated after the American Civil War. The legislation's mandate was, however, that any such immigrants be limited to those of Saxon heritage.

This book is a collection of stories that are told against a backdrop of the history of the early European and African migration to the South Carolina Lowcountry. While the history of the how the land was settled is important as a foundation for an appreciation of the essence of the Lowcountry, the truth of human existence emerges only when the lives of the people who have inhabited it mature with the landscape, and that combination defines the ever emerging character of the place. Put another way, the raw history of the settlement of the English colony of Carolina has long been read by the world in sanitized versions contained in the standard history books. But the truth, beyond the sanitized facts, often springs from human life.

These stories, some old and some new, reveal some of the truth about the life and the character and the soul of the Carolina Lowcountry in ways that cannot be fully understood and appreciated by reading the mere factual histories that have been written about it through the years. Place, people, and events added together create the scene, but in this case, the whole is much larger than its parts because together they create a depth of soul that defines the reality. The reality that has emerged is rich, and it includes the fundamental values of love, hate, rich, poor, justice, and injustice. The stories in this book are not sanitized and they present the struggles and foibles of real people.

A typical dictionary definition of the French word *terroir* is local or land. The real meaning of the word though is much broader and deeper. The word has a philosophical grounding: it is everything about what comes from the soil, especially grapes from which wine is made. *Terroir* includes cultivation methods, climate, temperature, and the quality of the people providing the labor to grow the crop, and the culture of the place. It alludes to the indefinable, ethereal quality that encompasses all of the elements working together to produce the quality, like the wine, of life itself. The result is a rich and unique mixture that the stories in this book illustrate about the people and the land of the Carolina Lowcountry.

The stories that follow the three immigration traditions naturally flow from the bare platform of history about what happened when people came to the Carolina Lowcountry. Some of the stories are old and embedded in history, while others are about recent events. All of them are intended, as described by Faulkner in his Nobel Prize address, to teach us about the mysteries and struggles of the human heart in conflict with itself. All of them are grounded in truth.

CAROLINA SUNRISE

THE SETTING
FROM THE DEPTHS

And God saw all that he had made, and it was very good.
Genesis 1:31

The presence of human beings on our little globe is a relatively recent development. We consume but an infinitesimal sliver on a pie-crust graph of life on the planet called Earth.

The account of creation in Genesis tells us that in the beginning, Earth was a dark place entirely covered by water. On the Biblical timetable, it was not until the third day—not quite halfway through the week—that the land emerged from the sea. Humankind did not appear on the scene until much later, on the sixth day. Scientists tell us that it took billions of years after the beginning of the formation of the terrestrial ball to get to that sixth day when a creature that could be called human came into being. But either way, eventually, as the American *Book of Common Prayer* proclaims, the Earth became our island home in the midst of the vastness of interstellar space. Nothing more than a tiny dot in time and space.

The land now called South Carolina is shaped much like an equilateral triangle, and lies on the coast of the Atlantic Ocean in the southeastern part of the continent of North America. It was not described that way until after European  explorers discovered the continent in the 15th and 16th centuries of the Christian Era. They commissioned cartographers to draw maps of the land they had found and to give place names to the geographic features they put on paper for the first time.

When the European explorers first set foot on the mainland of North America, they found a plain of flat land along the South Carolina coast. It had risen from the depths of the ocean and been exposed by the sea as it receded over thousands of years.

It is that plain that came to be known as the Carolina Lowcountry. It was first put into a Western European historical context by the early Spanish, French, and English explorers who began to appear there in small numbers. Sent by European monarchs seeking economic development opportunities in the new world, the explorers' task was to perform due-diligence investigations for the kingdoms they represented. They were the Chambers of Commerce of the day.

They saw the newly discovered Carolina Lowcountry and lands to the west as the emerging frontier for development opportunities for themselves and for the European monarchs who had sent them.

Little is known, even today, about the human inhabitants who greeted the first explorers. The Europeans called them Indians as they were under the mistaken impression that they were on the sub-continent. In any case, when the Europeans arrive, these Indians lived on the emerging coastal plain. But historians and anthropologists now agree that thousands of years earlier, their ancestors likely ventured across the Arctic reaches from Asia and Europe and gradually migrated to the southern extremes of what would become North America.

Almost 1,700 years into the Christian Era, the English monarch, Charles II—called *Carolus* in Latin—granted a charter to a group of his subjects for the development of a colony on the southeastern shore of North America to extend westward across the continent to the Pacific Ocean. In the 16th century, the intent of the European national powers was to open new land for agricultural and commercial enterprises. Some of their colonies on Atlantic and Caribbean islands just to the east of the vast newly-discovered continent were reaching their capacity of people and cultivated land. In the lingo used by modern real estate developers, some of the colonies, like Barbados, were almost "built out."

The English developers wanted to establish a claim to the newly-discovered land of North America before their European competitors. They could invest relatively small amounts of capital to make the new territory livable for the colonists they planned to recruit—men and women who would grow agricultural products and develop trade for their benefit. The developers thought that the settlement of this new land would be financially rewarding for them because they could supply food and other goods produced by the colonists to people at home at substantial profit.

The colonial developers named the new colony "Carolina" to honor their benefactor, the king, who had given them this magnificent opportunity. Early on, the land known as Carolina was divided into two sections—North Carolina and South Carolina—to make it easier for them to manage the royal spoils and to allow the vast colonial development to proceed under separate charters. Under this scenario, development could occur at a faster pace.

Geographers would describe the location of the Lowcountry as lying roughly about between latitude 33°22'N, 79°38'W and 32°30'N, and longitude 81°6'N and 81°6'W, which parallels the coastline. They would describe it as lying about on the same latitude as Egypt, a country in the north of the African continent.

The land of the Lowcountry generally lies along the eastern seaboard between the modern coastal cities of Georgetown—near the North Carolina state boundary on the north—and Hilton Head Island, near the Savannah River, on the south. Its western boundary is an irregular line that runs from northeast to southwest 75 to 100 miles inland from the modern coastline, a line that was once an ancient ocean high-water mark, hidden from human sight until the sea began to recede.

That line of demarcation between the old ocean and the high land is called the *fall line*. It is the point at which the upland rivers pour over onto the coastal plain on their way to the sea. The gently-sloping terraced plain eastward of the fall line, left dry as the sea gradually ebbed over the long course of time, is the paradise known as the Lowcountry.

Anyone who has experienced its fresh air and cool ocean breezes knows that the Carolina Lowcountry defies exact geographic definition. That's largely because the edges of its boundaries are not precise. For some, the Lowcountry is an amorphous state of being, especially precious to those inhabitants lucky enough to have been visited by the strong spirit that has lurked in the region throughout its history. Not everyone can see it or feel it, but those fortunate enough to experience it know it is a state of special grace and hope.

Several beautiful rivers end their course to the sea on Lowcountry shores. The Great Pee Dee and the Santee in the north, and the Broad and Savannah in the south, are the largest of them. Many smaller rivers also end their seaward journeys between Georgetown and Hilton Head Island—the Waccamaw, the Little Pee Dee, and the Black, all north of Charleston, with their black-colored water; and the Ashley, the Cooper, and the Stono, which surround the city of Charleston as they meander to the ocean.

In the south toward the Georgia state line, the Ashepoo, Combahee, and Edisto Rivers define the part of the Lowcountry known in modern times as the ACE Basin, an acronym made up from the first letters of the rivers that flow through it. In the late 20th century, the ACE Basin—an expanse of marshland lying between the high and low water levels of the ocean—was set aside for natural preservation and conservation.

The Basin's dimensions are set by the rising and falling tides. Most of it is covered by tall spartina and other species of grass that change colors with the seasons—in many shades of green and brown. The marshes are living and ever-growing ecosystems teeming with creatures from the air and sea—gulls, marsh hens, fish, oysters, shrimp, crabs, clams, and eels among them.

Palm trees, especially a species known locally as the "Palmetto," thrive along the coast. Among the many other trees indigenous to the Lowcountry are live oaks draped with Spanish moss, holly, and sweet gum—and cypress growing in shallow water.

These trees, along with other species of oak and pine (loblolly, short-leaf, and long-leaf) provide a canopy for smaller scrub oak, ferns, and other flora naturally found in sub-tropical climates. Sycamore, sweet gum, and elm are scattered throughout the area, as well as a variety bearing nuts and fruit—hickory, pecan, peach, plum.

Wildlife has always flourished throughout the Lowcountry. Birds, reptiles, and mammals have lived throughout the region in great numbers. Throughout history, for Native Americans, European colonizers and their progeny, whitetail deer, ducks of many varieties, wild turkeys, mourning doves, quail, and wild and feral hogs have provided hunters abundant bags of game year in and year out.

Egrets, cranes, cardinals, robins, sparrows, blue jays, bluebirds, and hawks are some of the predominant species of birds in highland regions of the Lowcountry. The coast is graced by gulls, ibises, ospreys, and brown pelicans among many other species of sea birds.

The inland rivers are full of fresh water fish. A fisherman in the Lowcountry's lakes, rivers, and streams can expect to catch bream, trout, bass, red breast, and rockfish. Blue crabs, shrimp, clams, scallops, and many varieties of fish are found in the coastal salt water.

In the 21st century, there are large numbers of alligators just inland from the tidal water. Among the saltwater fish in the ocean close to the shore and as far seaward as the Gulf Stream are tuna, grouper, sheepshead, snapper, shark, sword, trigger, sea bass, and dolphin.

Most species of animals that occupied the Lowcountry in the beginning of recorded history are still here, but some were unable to survive the imbalances in the natural order brought about by natural selection and human activity. The Carolina Parakeet, a beautiful subtropical bird, has become extinct in modern times, and the Ivory-Billed Woodpecker is no longer an inhabitant of the Lowcountry, though some think it may exist elsewhere on the continent.

Other animals, such as the Bald Eagle and the alligator, almost disappeared from the earth only to be nursed back from the edge of extinction in the late 20th century. The wild bobwhite quail, once an abundant game bird, is rarely found anymore, but fortunately, it has not yet gone the way of the Carolina parakeet. Its existence on earth is being artificially maintained by naturalists and game hunters.

The most obvious geologic change in the Lowcountry over time has been the ebb and flow of the ocean, slowly moving the line between the land and the sea along the ever-changing coastline. Throughout the history of man's occupation of the land, humans have tried to control the ocean's interaction with the coastline, but the ocean always wins the battle.

Human activity, though, has wrought the most immense changes to the Lowcountry landscape since its emergence from the sea. Geologic evidence shows that the first humans inhabited the Lowcountry about 12,000 years before the beginning of the Christian era when migrations from the north led men to it. It was about the year 1150 when writers began to document the first human settlements.

Little is known about the history and genealogy of these early humans. Modern anthropologists and historians say that about

2,700 descendants of the first humans—now known as Native Americans— resided in the Lowcountry at the beginning of the 21st Century. Some historians believe that a group called Mississippians were among the first to arrive from somewhere in the mid-western United States, perhaps from around present-day Illinois. These people organized a civilization called a chiefdom named *Cofitachequi*. The site of the central village of the chiefdom was on the northern edge of the Lowcountry—a little south of where the city of Camden is situated today. The chiefdom provided a governmental structure to the native population in and around the Lowcountry for centuries.

By the time Spanish explorers arrived in the coastal regions in the first half of the 16th century, there were over fifteen Indian nations in the Lowcountry. Near Charleston on the central Lowcountry coast were the Etiwan, Kiawah, Stono, Coosah, and the Edisto. To the north toward Georgetown were the Waccamaw, the Winyah, and the Pee Dee tribes. Around the modern city of Columbia, the state capital, the Wateree, Congaree, and Santee established inland nations along rivers that now carry their names. To the south, near Hilton Head Island, were the Ashepoo, Combahee, Escabracu, Kasihta, Wimbee, and the Westo.

These same tribal names are in still in use in the 21st century Lowcountry. Many modern commercial ventures bear the names of even other tribes of Native Americans who inhabited the place in pre-historic times. The Etiwan Fertilizer Company, with its logo of a fish being planted in the ground by a Native American, operated in and around Charleston until the mid-20th century, and the resort on a barrier island called Kiawah drew its name from the tribe that once inhabited it.

Not much is known about the languages spoken by the natives, but those occupying the coastal plain north of the Ashley River at Charleston generally spoke a language called Siouan, while those living south of the river spoke a language called Muskogean.

The arrival of Europeans was followed by the decimation and near extinction of the Indians. Their fate has now been recorded in written history, but little is known about their culture and the comings and goings of their daily lives in the early history.

In the early 16th century, there was competition among the European political powers, especially between the French and Spanish, as to as to which of them could first successfully establish colonial outposts along the southeastern North American continental coast.

The Spanish were the first to arrive in 1514 when Lucas Vasquez de Ayllón dispatched an exploratory party from his base of operations on the Caribbean island of Hispaniola to search for land where sugar could be grown. Following the positive reports from the first landward exploratory expedition, Ayllón sent another investigative party to the Carolina coast in 1521, and another in 1525.

Their conclusions were that huge amounts of land for the production of crops were there for the taking and that an abundant labor supply was available that was not only cheap but free. It was assumed that the people who lived on the land could be easily pressed into involuntary servitude. For example, it was during the 1521 expedition that some of the Native Americans were lured on board the ship, taken to Hispaniola, and sold into slavery, thus initiating a cultural and economic system for the development of the new world that has kept a significant portion of the population of the Lowcountry in economic shackles to the present day.

Those shackles were literal until September 22, 1862, when slavery was outlawed in the United States by the Emancipation Proclamation. The practice ended *de jure*, 341 years after its introduction by the Spanish explorers. But the insidious effects of slavery and its aftermath have continued — from its institution in the Lowcountry in 1521 until today.

Another long-reaching conclusion drawn by the first of the 16th-century explorers was that the vast lands of the Lowcountry and beyond were available for economic exploitation. Soil, water, trees, and other natural resources were there for anyone who could get to them, thus establishing another practice continued today by a host of developers.

The explorers of the 1525 expedition sent by Ayllón sighted a point of land on the Carolina coast on August 18th, which they named Santa Elena in honor of the saint honored on the liturgical calendar of the Roman Catholic Church. Perhaps the first European name given to any spot on the North American mainland, it is still called St. Helena. Located in Beaufort County on Parris Island. St. Helena sits a little north of Hilton Head Island.

Positive reports from those first two scouting parties led Ayllón to the formation of a colonizing party to establish a permanent settlement. According to Walter Edgar in *South Carolina, A History*, a seminal work of regional history, the first attempt at the colonization of the North American continent comprised six ships and 600 prospective settlers. The settlers, under the personal leadership of Ayllón set out from Hispaniola in the summer of 1526. They reached the yet unnamed Carolina mainland somewhere along the Lowcountry coast and put down the first colony in North America, naming it San Miguel de Guadalupe.

The colonization was short-lived. There was an almost immediate onset of disease of epidemic proportions, mutinies, a slave rebellion, and freezing weather. Ayllón himself died soon after the party arrived. His death and the challenges encountered by the proposed residents led to the failure of the colonization plan, and the settlement was abandoned before the end of the year. Only 150 of the original 600 settlers survived to return home.

Then, in 1540, Hernando De Soto led a Spanish expedition across modern-day South Carolina, skirting the western edges of the Lowcountry and continuing into the interior of the continent beyond the Mississippi River. His party comprised about 600 men including at least a dozen Roman Catholic priests.

Their route through the state took them across the Savannah River near the city of Augusta, Georgia, and then toward the present site of Columbia near the confluence of the Congaree and Wateree Rivers (where the two rivers form the Santee). From there they traveled north up the Wateree to the Indian town of Cofitachequi, found in the High Hills of Santee near the site of modern-day Camden.

De Soto and his men remained as the guests of the Indians for about two weeks before heading northward and westward into the Blue Ridge Mountains in North Carolina. In an act of bad faith and a breach of civilized hospitality, they took the Indian queen, the Cacica, and some other women of the tribe with them allegedly as guides, but held them as hostages to protect the expedition from attack by other Indians as they traveled westward.

De Soto's incursion was yet another attempt by the Spaniards to establish their influence in the land masses north of modern-day Florida where they had already established settlements. But De Soto would fail. He and his party withdrew from North America without establishing a colony—and it would be more than 25 years before Spain would again attempt to colonize the Lowcountry.

France entered the colonization competition just after the mid-16th century. The first of four historic waves of French immigration arrived in the Lowcountry on May 77, 1562, when two French ships under the command of Jean Ribaut, a Huguenot, sailed into a beautiful bay they named Port Royal. The party comprised about 150 men, and they established a colony near the site of Spain's Santa Elena, calling it Charlesfort to honor Charles IX, the French king. Ribaut's party built a small fort to protect them from the Indians and from the expected Spanish incursions.

It is thought that most of the men on these ships were, like Jean Ribaut, Huguenots who wished to escape the raging religious wars in western France. The Huguenots were a good source of recruits for the mission to colonize Carolina, as it would allow them to avoid religious restrictions at home. It was not until 1598, 26 years later, that Henry IV proclaimed the Edict of Nantes, ending the Roman Catholic persecution of French Protestants for almost a century. (The Edict would be revoked by the Edict of Fountainbleu in 1685.)

Other reasons put forward by historians for the founding of Charlesfort was the desire of France to compete with Spanish plans to colonize the territory north of Florida and to be able to monitor and intercept Spanish cargo ships sailing along the Carolina coast as they were about to tum eastward to make the Atlantic crossing.

After about a month at the fort, Ribaut left for France with his two ships to get more supplies for the new colony, leaving Albert de La Pierria in command at the fort, supported by around 27 men. Ribaut's plans for an early return were thwarted, however, when the ongoing religious wars in France prevented his entry into the harbor at Le Havre. When he arrived there, conditions at home were such that he was not able to return to America.

On the other side of the Atlantic, conditions at the fort rapidly deteriorated soon after in Ribaut's departure. The men mutinied and killed La Pierria, deciding to build a ship to cross the Atlantic and make for home, leaving one man behind with the Edisto Indians.

There were few survivors on board the crude vessel when it was encountered off the coast of England. The French, too, had failed to establish a permanent colony in the Lowcountry.

The Spanish made another attempt to colonize the Lowcountry in early 1566 when they established another settlement at Santa Elena. Concerned that the French were again planning to challenge their right to what they considered to be Spanish territory, the Spanish King, Philip II, granted a charter to Pedro Menéndez de Avilés to occupy the region. Menéndez chose Santa Elena because it was near the abandoned Charlesfort. His proximity to the attempted French colony would make it easier for him to repel future invasion attempts by the French.

As with other Europeans, the arrangement between the Spanish king and Menéndez was a commercial venture to promote the development of Spain's interests in the New World. While the king wished to assure Spain's dominance in the region, Menéndez's goal was to profit from the economics of the venture, as any commercial developer would wish to do. For him, the king's commission was an extraordinary opportunity to manage the development of North America for himself as well. There were many opportunities open to him to make money as he arranged for the immigration of settlers, created towns and forts to protect them from the surrounding Indians, and developed agriculture leading to exports of food and other commodities to Spain.

The agreement with Philip required Menéndez to begin the Lowcountry colony with at least 100 farmers and expand the number of farmers to 400 within three years. The plan took hold, and by 1569, there were about 200 people in the settlement. The town of Santa Elena was organized around forty houses built under Menéndez's direction, and it became the capital of Spanish Florida. In addition to farmers, Menéndez arranged for Jesuit priests to come to tend to their spiritual health and to conduct missionary activities among the Indians living nearby. Right away the colonists began raising corn, barley, melons, squash, grapes, and green vegetables to support the town. They also established herds of livestock including cows and hogs.

The first fort at Santa Elena was called San Salvador. In 1566, it was replaced by the larger San Filipe, intended to provide added protection against the bellicose Indian population. This new fort was occupied by 250 men brought from Spain by Juan Pardo.

Pardo conducted a couple of expeditionary trips from Santa Elena into the interior of the continent but never penetrated beyond the Appalachian Mountains. He had hoped to find a westward route to Mexico and, at the same time, create friendly relations with the Indians. He failed to achieve either goal.

Although the venture was initially successful, that success was short-lived. Supplies from Europe were hard to come by and within four or five years, diseases of epidemic proportions were prevalent. Menéndez died in 1574 while on a trip to Spain, and the responsibility for the government of the colony was assumed by his son-in-law, Don Diego de Velasco, and later by Hernando de Miranda, who was married to Menéndez's daughter Catalina. Catalina herself inherited her father's title as Adelantado of Florida.

The fort, San Filipe, and the town at Santa Elena were burned by Indians in 1577. Fighting led to the deaths of some of the soldiers defending the fort, and to the brief abandonment of Santa Elena.

During the hiatus, a French ship ran aground in the sound at Port Royal. Indians, mistaking the interlopers for Spaniards, attacked the fortification built by the survivors of the shipwreck. But when they discovered that they were French settlers, they withdrew and welcomed them. The eventual fate of the shipwrecked Frenchmen, however, is unknown.

Yet another group of would-be Spanish settlers arrived at Santa Elena in 1577, this time a military force led by Pedro Menéndez Margués. Their plan was to again build a fortification for protection against the Indians. The fort, to be called San Marcos, was prefabricated in Saint Augustine and brought on shipboard to Santa Elena and constructed on the site in six days.

It took the occupants of San Marcos about a year to exact the revenge they sought, and to subdue the Indians who had been responsible for the destruction of Fort San Filipe and the town of

Santa Elena. Settlers returned, and by 1580, there were about 400 people living there. During this period, the town was the only significant post in Spanish America. Saint Augustine, Spain's capital of Florida for most of the time of its occupation of the Lowcountry and points south, had been temporarily evacuated after it was attacked and destroyed by an English fleet under the command of Sir Francis Drake in June 1586.

The town of Santa Elena was abandoned again in the summer of 1587 when the Spanish decided to consolidate all their resources on the eastern shore of North America at Saint Augustine.

The Spanish never again occupied Santa Elena. The rivalry between Spain and France for hegemony in the New World kept the possibility for the establishment of an enduring colony on the Lowcountry coast open from 1514 till 1587, but by century's end, no established European settlements existed in the Lowcountry. Obstacles encountered by the Spanish and French settlers prevented a permanent settlement from taking root.

The lack of a dependable supply line to the mother country to ensure vital supplies of food, medicine, and clothing; the inability to control disease; and an inadequate armed force for protection from the Indians who occupied the land the Europeans wished to settle made it impossible to establish a permanent, self-perpetuating colony. Almost a century would pass before new attempts were made to colonize this rich land when an Englishman named Alexander Parris acquired it in 1715.

In 1891, Santa Elena—now known as Parris Island—became a military post of the United States Marine Corps. Twenty-five years later, on November 1, 1915, the post was designated as a basic training station and from then until now, it has been known as the Marine Corps Recruit Depot.

The first permanent European Lowcountry settlement was finally established in 1670, named for Charles II of England, who had chartered the company of Englishmen to plan and execute the development of the colony that also bore his name. That city, first known as Charles Towne and then Charleston after the American Revolution, lies on the coastline about midway between the northern and southern extreme. It became the cultural and spiritual center of the colonial population soon after its founding.

Many elements—air, water, climate, animal, mineral, and perhaps the most important one, a rich diversity of people from many lands— all came together to form the essence of this coastal plain in a way that no king or real estate developer could ever have predicted or planned. Beginning its formation billions of years before the dawn of human existence on the planet, this ever-distilling mixture continues to nurture and sustain the richness of the ethos that is the Lowcountry.

PART I

ONE

THE ENGLISH

"…the hand of God was eminently seen in thinning the Indians to make room for the English."

John Archdale, Governor of the colony of Carolina, 1695

A new chapter in the race to the frontier began when Charles I, the English king, granted his subject, Sir Robert Heath, a charter to develop land in North America. The grant, beginning on the coast of the Atlantic Ocean, ran from the southern border of the colony of Virginia to the north to the Saint Mary's River in what later became the colony of Georgia to the south, and stretched westward to the Pacific Ocean.

The year was 1629. The charter was England's challenge to the historic and persistent claims of Spain and France to the territory. Heath and his colleagues named the land Carolina to honor their beneficent king.

Sir Robert sent an exploratory expedition to the territory to assess and evaluate its potential for development. But the explorers were so ill-equipped and inexperienced that they never made it to the lands of Carolina. They landed, instead, in Virginia, and then inexplicably returned to England without laying eyes on the land they went to see. Frustrated by the failure of the expedition, Heath's company dropped the idea of establishing a colony on the North American continent and set their sights on more modest proposals to develop some of the Atlantic and Caribbean islands. They began to focus their attention on Barbados, where a plan of colonization was already in progress.

The decision by these Englishmen—to lower their sights to concentrate on the development of relatively small ocean islands— proved to be a wise one. They discovered that the plan to develop Barbados allayed many of the difficult problems of a broader continental development. The persistent problem for the Europeans— Spanish, French, and English—had been the inability to provide vital supplies and other support from their home bases across the Atlantic Ocean.

Barbados lies on the dividing line between the Caribbean Sea and the Atlantic Ocean, about 175 kilometers east of St. Lucia and St. Vincent, and 200 kilometers northeast of Tobago. It is 21 miles long, 14 wide, and 1,000 feet above the level of the ocean at its highest point. With its temperate climate and rich, arable land, the island would be able to supply agricultural products to England; it would be a sort of a farm away from home.

The developers reasoned that an island such as Barbados could be more easily supplied and defended against interlopers and native insurgents and that a successful well-provisioned permanent island settlement could serve as a base of operations for future continental expansion.

The first exploratory visitors, led by Captain James Powell, arrived on the island on May 14, 1625, to investigate the feasibility of establishing a colony. A report from Powell to Charles I led to the grant of a royal patent to James Hay, the first earl of Carlisle, as a Lord Proprietor to establish a colony on Barbados.

Hay's plan was to organize an agricultural colony to grow tobacco for export to England. The first colonists, 80 in number, arrived from the mother country in February 1627, aboard four ships. More than half of the first settlers were indentured servants who agreed to work for the development company for seven years (five years for those under 21) after their arrival on the island.

In the early years following the first settlement, grants were issued by the Lord Proprietor, each bestowing land ownership on some of the colonists. Soon after, political restlessness among these land-owning colonists arose. Based on the English model, a representative general assembly was organized in 1639 to manage this restlessness. Also reflecting the English model, the Church of England became the established church, and the island was divided into 11 parishes to provide public, political, and religious governmental structures.

Unfortunately, the plan to grow and export tobacco did not succeed because the quality of the product was inferior to that grown in other Caribbean colonies. As a result, in 1630, there was a shift in the Barbadian agricultural plan from tobacco planting to the cultivation of cotton.

The quality of the cotton produced on the Barbadian land was excellent, and all of it was exported to England at fair prices. The cotton crops were so abundant and of such high quality that the island's economy grew and flourished until 1639.

But the success of the cotton planters soon led to their failure—it created an over-supply of the crop on the London markets and prices plummeted, sending the Barbadian economy into a collapse.

Barbadian farmers then turned to the cultivation of other crops: first to indigo until 1643, and then to sugar. The sugar industry and other economic endeavors spawned by it have fueled the island economy ever since. Barbadian rum—said to be the best in the world because of the abundance of sugar—has helped maintain the economic health and good spirits of the Barbadian people throughout the island's history.

The governance by the proprietorship on the island ended in the 1660s when Barbados became a British crown colony. From then until now, the island's government has been directed from London.

There were over 11,000 landowners in Barbados in 1645, but that number diminished to only 745 by 1667. The significant reduction in the number of landowners was brought about by the consolidation of land holdings by large plantation owners as the population continued to grow. By 1670, all the arable land on Barbados was used for sugar production, and there was no land remaining on the island for the future expansion of the plantation system.

The initial settlement plan had not proposed the use of slaves to support the economy, but in the early days of the island's colonization, Henry Powell, an English island farmer, acquired ten African slaves to work on his plantation. His introduction of slaves to Barbados was likely the first step in the development of the European-Atlantic slave trade, and the institution soon became a full-blown feature of the island economy. Western European nations embarked on a course of supplanting the prevalent colonial system of indentured servitude—itself a form of slavery—with a more oppressive, evil, and destructive system of human bondage. The Dutch became the largest suppliers of slaves to the New World, and Barbados was a major recipient of their slave cargoes.

It is not known with certainty where in Africa the Barbadian slaves came from, but historians now believe that most of them were captured in west Africa, probably in Ghana, and brought to places all over the Caribbean. By 1666, there were 50,000 slaves of African origin in Barbados alone. The slaves became an essential ingredient of the robust Barbadian agricultural economy that lined the pockets of the local farmers. The system was even more valuable to the London merchants as the minimal costs to support the slave labor force helped control the costs to produce the crops and the prices they had to pay for them. Before the end of the 17th century, over 135,000 slaves were imported, mostly from Africa.

But Barbados was not alone. Slavery became the bedrock of the success of the colonial economy all over the New World until it was abolished in the late 19th century in England and in America. The demonizing spiritual and physical effects of slavery still haunt every place where it was practiced, and it naturally burdens those whose forefathers endured its destructive forces.

The lack of land on the island to expand the sugar production led to the emigration of many small planters seeking new economic opportunities. There were 2,000 emigrations to other colonies in the year 1670, and it is thought that at least another 1,000 left before the end of the century.

Charles II acceded to the throne in 1660, thus ending the English Civil War and the eleven-year regime of Oliver Cromwell. The restoration of royal authority in England made it possible for many of those exiled by the Cromwell regime to the return home.

One of those returning was Sir John Colleton who had spent the time of the civil war in Barbados. Armed with the knowledge of the need for colonial expansion beyond Barbados, and the desire to be rewarded for his unwavering loyalty to the crown during the bad times of the Civil War in England, he began to lobby for rights to colonize continental North America.

Colleton had a vision that the march to the next frontier of development in the New World would lead to unprecedented economic expansion, and to great wealth for him and those he recruited to join him in this new venture. Colleton knew that there was no more land to develop on Barbados and that it was time for those with a vision of the future to move on. He believed that the London markets had the capacity to take in all the goods that new North American colonies could produce, and so he assembled a group of influential men in London to join him in a petition to Charles II seeking a royal charter to develop Carolina. As they all held important government posts, they likewise had close and powerful connections to the king and government.

The seven men assembled by Colleton to join him in the colonial venture included Anthony Ashley Cooper, chancellor of the exchequer and later the first earl of Shaftesbury; John, Lord Berkeley, a member of the Privy Council; George Carteret, a chamberlain of the royal household; Edward Hyde, earl of Clarendon, the prime minister; George Monck, duke of Albemarle; William Craven, earl of

Craven, a member with some of the others of the Council for Foreign Plantations; and Sir William Berkeley, the royal governor of Virginia.

The Lords Proprietors were given their charter on March 24, 1663 to develop the land—the same as had been given to Heath—from Virginia to the north to Spanish Florida in the south, and extending from the Atlantic Ocean on the east to the Pacific Ocean in the west. Their initial investment was a modest $5,000 each as measured in modern American currency.

The royal charter gave the group of colonial developers essentially the same powers that the sovereign possessed in other colonial territories, and they all believed the potential for profit was enormous. The authority they acquired for the venture included the rights to impose and collect taxes, raise an army, impose fees whenever they desired for any colonial activity, establish towns and governmental structures, and export goods duty-free to England for seven years.

It took the Lords Proprietors a few years to lay the groundwork for the project. In the meantime, Sir John Colleton died in 1666, and Sir William Berkeley returned to Virginia. Anthony Ashley Cooper became the leader of the remaining group of Proprietors, each of which would contribute an additional $37,000 each toward the capital costs of the venture, and he began to organize them for action.

In 1668, as they were finalizing the plans for the voyage to Carolina, the group petitioned for another royal charter to develop the islands of the Bahamas with the same authority bestowed on them for the development of Carolina. The new petition was granted, and they received a charter for the Bahamas development in 1670.

Three years earlier, the group sent Captain William Sayle to Carolina to once again try to determine the feasibility of sending out permanent settlers. Sayle sailed up and down the southeast Atlantic coast and reported that there were numerous rivers flowing into the sea from the coastal plain, that the land he saw was heavily forested, and that the terrain all along the seacoast was flat. But he didn't go onto the land because of the presence of what he described as "hostile savages" who appeared whenever he attempted to make a landfall. On the basis of what he said, plans proceeded to organize the colonization of the land of Carolina.

The new leader of the Proprietors, Anthony Ashley Cooper, now the first earl of Shaftesbury, was born in 1621 at Wimborne St. Giles in England. Like his predecessor Colleton, he was a Barbados plantation owner, but he never lived there.

Ashley Cooper assigned his personal secretary, John Locke, the job of developing a structure of government for the new colony. Locke drafted a document he entitled "Fundamental Constitutions of Carolina," which Cooper and the other Lords Proprietors proposed as the basis for the colony's government. Locke's Fundamental Constitutions were never formally enacted by the settlers or imposed on the colony, but many of its visionary elements were, in fact, implemented as a part of the colonial government.

In matters of religion, the Locke proposals invited and allowed all western religions into the colony *except Roman Catholics*. The significant exclusion of Roman Catholics reflected the European political issues of the day. It was a discriminatory policy that endured until the American Revolution and ratification of the United States Constitution in 1789, which guaranteed freedom of religion to everyone—including Roman Catholics.

Locke's *Fundamental Constitutions* also inculcated the institution of slavery by a clause in the document: *"Every freeman of Carolina shall have absolute power and authority over his negro slaves..."*

Continuing his plan to move the project forward without delay, Ashley Cooper acquired, outfitted, and manned three ships to take the first settlers to the Carolina Lowcountry in 1669. The vessels were named Albemarle, Carolina, and Port Royal, names that would become important in South Carolina and remain so throughout its long history. Captain Joseph West, an experienced colonial leader, was put in charge of the seagoing venture.

The three ships left England in the summer of 1669 and made their first stop at Kinsale, in Ireland, to try to enlist more settlers for the Carolina colony. But recruitment proved unsuccessful, and after a period, they sailed from Kinsale for Barbados. A voyage of about six weeks in reasonable weather, they finally made port at Bridgetown in October. Two of the ships returned to England, leaving the first settlers until February 26, 1670, when the first group of English colonists sailed for Carolina. Again, there were three ships in the fleet—the Carolina, the Port Royal, and a new ship called The Three Brothers, which replaced the Albemarle, which was lost in a storm while in port on Barbados.

The Carolina made landfall on March 15th at Bull's Bay on the Carolina coast, about thirty miles north of where they eventually established their settlement at Charles Towne. The plan had been to settle at Port Royal, near the old colony at Santa Elena, but the chief of the Kiawah tribe persuaded them to instead establish the colony on Old Town Creek, which led from the west bank of the Ashley River.

The other two ships in the fleet never made it to Carolina. The Port Royal ran into a shoal in the Bahama Islands from which it could not be floated and The Three Brothers was driven to the Virginia coast by a storm encountered on a trip northward from the Bahamas. It was fortunate for the venture that most of the settlers—130 of them—were aboard the Carolina.

There were few Barbadians in the first group of settlers, but in the ensuing years, the majority of new arrivals came from the island, bringing with them African slaves in increasing numbers. Some of the later Carolina settlers came from other British colonial islands including Bermuda, the Bahamas, and Nevis.

This settlement, unlike earlier colonizing attempts by the Spanish, took root and was sustained because it was supported by the commercial venture of the Lords Proprietors. In military terms, the supply lines to the base in Barbados and in England were kept intact and were nourished, and the settlers and their slaves at Charles Town were understood to be vitally important to the success of the Proprietors' economically-based enterprise.

The English plan for the development of the colony of Carolina had a secondary purpose, that of easing the overpopulated and over-planted island of Barbados. It also allowed the Crown to reward some of its strongest and most powerful supporters by making them Lords Proprietors of a huge piece of real estate from which they had the opportunity to make personal fortunes. It was, they thought, divinely inspired and protected just as the Crown itself.

According to Dr. David Ramsay in his 1858 *History of South Carolina,* John Archdale, a governor of the colony in 1695, reported that the Indian population in the two decades following the settlement of Carolina had been made easier to deal with and to subdue by God's friendly intervention on their behalf. Archdale wrote:

"...in the first settlement of Carolina, the hand of God was eminently seen in thinning the Indians to make room for the English..." and "...it pleased Almighty God to send unusual sicknesses amongst them as the small pox, to lessen their numbers so that the English, in comparison to the Spaniards, have but little blood to answer for."

The new settlement reflected much of the colonial structure that had earlier developed in the settlements on Barbados. Eleven parishes on Barbados provided the political and religious structure for the colonial organization. Nine of the parish names were borrowed for the first parishes in the Carolina colony—St. Michael, St. Philip, St. Peter, St. Thomas, Christ Church, St. John, St. James, St. George, and St. Andrew. All nine continue as names of parishes in the Episcopal Church, successor to the Church of England in South Carolina. Some still identify geographical areas of the Lowcountry even today.

Although some of the Spanish and French place names are still in use around Beaufort and Hilton Head Island (St. Helena, Port Royal, Calibogue, Ribault), the new English colony established itself using the names of its patrons. Early in the colonial history, four counties were established and named to honor four of the Lords Proprietors. They were Carteret, Craven, Berkeley, and Colleton, the last two of which are still in use. The most active Lord Proprietor, Anthony Ashley Cooper, is honored by having the most prominent rivers in the center of the Lowcountry coast named for him.

Some say the Ashley and Cooper Rivers come together from either side of the Charleston peninsula to join in Charleston Harbor to form the Atlantic Ocean. They do in fact come together in the harbor and then run their courses into the ocean. Off the peninsula, the land to the east is called East of the Cooper, and the space in the other direction is known as West of the Ashley. Untold numbers of streets and establishments all over the Lowcountry bear one of his names.

An inn on Broad Street in Charleston is named the John Rutledge House Inn in honor of its first owner, John Rutledge, the first governor of the state, who would also become the Chief Justice of the United States. The house was built for him in 1765 by his family after his return from studying law at the Middle Temple in London. Behind the main house, as a part of the modern inn, are two "wing" houses for guests—the Ashley on the west side and the Cooper on the east. The two rivers are about a half mile in each direction.

The colonists and Lords Proprietors prospered for many years. The first permanent institutions put in place endured. But there came a time in 1719, after a few years of bickering, when colonists, fed up with the Proprietors who were their patrons and company managers, demanded a royal government, and with it the rights and privileges accorded to *all* subjects of the British Empire.

Although they had been given reasonable freedom to handle their own colonial affairs, the local people, after 49 years of private commercial leadership, decided that it was time for a change. They effectively threw out the Lords Proprietors by the end of 1719, and installed a colonial government under the rule of George I. The royal colonial system prevailed in Carolina for another 50 years or so until the mid 1770s when the local leadership, now more widespread and in concert with other American colonies, again became disenchanted with their absentee authority and declared themselves to be a united people free of government from across the sea.

The path to that freedom began in earnest when the first defining battle of the American Revolution was fought on June 28, 1776, in Charleston Harbor, in the heart of the Lowcountry. The colonists at Fort Sullivan, under the command of Colonel William Moultrie, miraculously sank most of the British fleet, commanded by Sir Peter Parker, as it rested at anchor in the waters just off the shoreline. It was the first of three defining battles of the Revolution, followed by two other such engagements in later years at Saratoga and Yorktown. Six days later, the Declaration of Independence was signed and the war of revolution officially began. Despite the inclination in American history classes to focus on the northeastern states' involvement in the war, it is surmised that more military engagements were fought in South Carolina and in the Lowcountry than in any other of the British colonies in North America.

As the independent and "united" country came into its own, the road that led from the colonial days when the English crown ruled the affairs of the Lowcountry was not a smooth one. There were arguments between the separate colonies of mid-North America about what kind of government they needed and wanted. An overriding issue was the authority that should be retained by the individual states as opposed to the power given to the central government.

Thomas Jefferson did not at first favor the constitutional plan. His principal objection was that the constitutional document gave too much authority to the federal government. Jefferson's belief was that the federal government should be given authority to conduct the foreign policy of the new nation and that all other governmental functions should be conducted by the individual states as they wished on their own terms. His objections were assuaged only by an agreement to append the first ten amendments that he drafted to the constitution thus guaranteeing specified individual rights to the people of the young nation. Some believe that the most important of Jefferson's proposed constitutional amendments is the very first one that provides for freedom of religion and freedom of speech to every citizen of the United States. It was in this mode that the Lowcountry, as a part of the new nation, began to drift away from its English roots that had first been planted more than 100 years earlier.

A settlement was reached on the issue, and a government prescribed by the United States Constitution was ratified in 1789. The new nation then began to function as a unified system of self-governance.

Although the English crown no longer controlled the government of the 13 American colonies, much of the British culture remained in the Lowcountry and throughout the land. English remained the common language in South Carolina and in all the other former colonies. Many of the governmental, religious, and social institutions in the Lowcountry are still influenced by those established by the Lords Proprietors and the English crown in the 17th and 18th centuries.

In addition, the legal institutions of the Lowcountry and elsewhere were developed on models of English procedure and law. The traditions of the English common law still prevail in the Lowcountry, even in the 21st century. In South Carolina, the statutory law of the state provides that if the law applicable to a particular situation that is presented in a state court cannot be resolved by the application of existing statutory law, or by reference to precedential case law, it must be decided then by the application of the English Common Law.

Some of the procedures used in the Lowcountry's criminal courts, as well as in courts throughout South Carolina, are the same in the 21st century as when the English crown operated the local justice system in colonial days.

An example of the archaic procedure is found in the language used when a prisoner charged with the commission of a felony is arraigned in court. The prisoner is instructed to stand before a court official who asks the prisoner to affirm his name and to raise his right hand. The prisoner, then, on all such occasions, dutifully raises his right hand, and the court official, usually the clerk of the court, immediately says, "put it down."

This curious ritual has nothing whatever to do with anything that is relevant to the upcoming trial of the prisoner. Its significance is generally unknown to anyone involved in the act of performing it or to those observing it, but the reason the prisoner is asked to raise his right hand, identify himself, and then put his hand down is to allow the court to determine if he had previously relied upon the old English criminal defense called "benefit of clergy."

In the English governmental system, at home and in its colonies, church and state were joined. There was a court where criminal charges could be brought against anyone. But there was also a separate court where crimes charged against members of the clergy could be resolved. The clerical or ecclesiastical courts were generally more lenient that the secular ones. So, if a criminal defendant could establish that he was a member of the clergy, on whatever definition applied at the time, then that person could exercise his right to be tried in the clerical court by claiming the "benefit of clergy," and be assured of a lighter sentence or none at all.

The only hitch was that a member of the clergy was allowed to claim this valuable right *only once*. To make a record of the claim of the ecclesiastical right, the court ordered that the palm of the clergyman's right hand be branded with a hot iron. This formed an unmistakable scar that, when observed by the clerk of court, established that the prisoner was not entitled to claim the benefit of clergy, and would have to settle for the harsher sentence awaiting him. So far as it is known, no such right has been claimed by any defendant in the courts of the Lowcountry in well over 200 years, but the ties to the mother country are still quite unconsciously retained in this quaint way.

The established church in the Lowcountry before the American Revolution was The Church of England, the head of which—then and now—is the English sovereign. It had been so since Henry VIII, the English king who broke communion with the Roman Catholic Church because the Pope would not permit his marriage following a divorce. Henry declared himself to be head of the Church instead, and so it has been ever since. The English sovereign is the head of the Church of England, and the sovereign's chief surrogate for the operation of the Church is the Archbishop of Canterbury.

The government established in the Lowcountry by the Lords Proprietors, and later by the English crown, was tolerant of the existence of other religious traditions in the colony, e.g., Baptists, Presbyterians, etc., with one important exception. No Roman Catholic was allowed by Locke's Constitutions.

In fact, no Roman Catholic was allowed to immigrate to Carolina until after the disestablishment of the Church of England during the American Revolution. After the disestablishment of a state church in the colonies, the successor to The Church of England became known as The Protestant Episcopal Church in the United States of America or simply The Episcopal Church. The institution has carried itself forward using many of the old colonial church buildings, a liturgy prescribed by *The Book of Common Prayer*—first written in 1549 in England—and has maintained a spiritual tie to the see of Canterbury via an organization known as The Anglican Communion.

The separation from the mother country was not peaceful even after the end of the American Revolution. Less than a generation from the beginning of the new government, a dispute arose with England that resulted in the War of 1812. The issues igniting that war involved freedom of movement on the high seas.

The British, flexing their power and dominance on the world's oceans, engaged in a pattern of interference with and harassment of American shipping interests. The war did not last long, although major battles were fought on home soil in Washington and New Orleans. For many American diplomats abroad, the war began and ended before they could even report the hostilities in their host countries.

Unlike during the Revolution, the Lowcountry was largely unaffected by the War of 1812. Notwithstanding Pearl Harbor and 9/11, that war would be the last time forces of a foreign government fought battles on American soil.

Except for the necessity of defending itself in the 1812 war, the Lowcountry and the rest of the Carolina colony had conducted its affairs free of interference from the mother country, although its future was influenced by the development of trade between merchants in England and the northern states where the textile industry was centered.

However, just a few years after the War of 1812, a "nullification" controversy began to heat up. The northern states, holding a majority of the votes in the Congress, insisted upon imposing onerous tariffs on cotton to make it economically impossible for the southern states to sell their cotton to the English mills. As a result, Lowcountry farmers were forced to sell their cotton to mills in Massachusetts at artificially low prices. The only solution was to ignore or "nullify" the laws preventing the sale of cotton to the English.

Another issue advanced by the north was the abolition of slavery, which was inextricably bound to economic concerns. Neither cotton nor rice could be produced without the use of slave labor. These two pressures eventually led to the American Civil War, and South Carolina led the way.

The state secession convention met in a hall at 134 Meeting Street in Charleston on December 20, 1860. James Louis Petigru, a resident of the city and a great lawyer was walking with an ardent unionist along Meeting Street opposite the convention site when the secession vote was about to be taken. A young man stopped them to ask what was going on in the hall across the street. Petigru is alleged to have said, "In my opinion, South Carolina is too small to be a republic and too large to be a lunatic asylum."

The secession vote, however, was unanimous.

The horrible war began in earnest four months later, when on April 12, 1861, Fort Sumter, which was occupied by federal troops, was bombarded by forces of the Confederate States of America. The siege lasted for two days before the Union troops evacuated the fort.

Of course, the war steadily intensified and wrought hundreds of thousands of deaths—perhaps as many as 800,000—over four years of fighting. Peace finally came, but the Lowcountry—and the rest of the states that comprised the Confederacy—was physically, spiritually, and economically devastated, a condition from which it would not fully recover until the mid-20th century. The English had attempted to help the Confederates during the War, hoping to be able to revive their earlier trade in agricultural products. But they were not helpful enough to swing the balance of power against superior northern resources.

Even so, since the end of the Civil War, England has been an ally of the United States in many wars and conflicts, including both World Wars, Korea, Vietnam, and the Iraqi invasion in 2003.

The Lowcountry has been part of a free and independent state now for over 200 years, subject only to the laws of God, the Constitution of the United States, and its own strong free will. South Carolina has always had a mind of its own. There are today frequent reminders of the founders that can be seen in surviving place names, in the influence of many institutions that add to its civic and culture life, in the behavior of people in their comings and goings, and in the everyday turning of the pages of history.

As the sun rises and sets each new day in South Carolina, the essence of the state can be summed up in what Gail Collins wrote in *The New York Times* on February 22, 2000: "Look, it's an unusual place. Half of American history involves efforts to get South Carolina to stop acting out."

TWO
G. L. HALL

The city of Charleston, where the colony was anchored, is probably the most English feeling and looking place in the United States. The prevailing 21st-century architectural style is almost entirely a product of the 18th century.

The result is that even today, people arriving from the mother country feel a real touch of "home." Although the English haven't occupied the land as a governing force since the end of the American Revolution, there have always been a few English people around, like the Shaftesburys, who visit to check on their colonial investment.

Most of the English visitors to the Lowcountry have been tourists, but occasionally they have come to stay. Such was the case for Gordon Langley Hall, who arrived in the early 1960s. He bought a house right away at 56 Society Street and settled into life in the city. This urbane and charming English author claimed Sissinghurst, the estate of the Nicolson family in Kent—where the likes of Virginia Woolf and Vita

Sackville-West and her husband Harold Nicolson were prominent inhabitants—as his native home. Mr. Hall pointed to the actress Dame Margaret Rutherford as his adoptive mother and godmother.

Hall's introduction caused quite a stir in a city that prided itself on the high quality of its urbanity (interpreted by some living elsewhere in the former colony as arrogance), a city which less than a century earlier had endured the horrors of the Civil War, a city that had suffered the effects of a devastating earthquake in 1886. The unexpected arrival of this newcomer who, by all appearances, was a proper English gentleman, hit Charleston with a big bang that reverberated in every nook and cranny of the old city and is still a topic of quiet conversation in some of the downtown precincts.

He seemed to be the epitome of a gentleman one imagines exists only in the most exclusive gentlemen's clubs in London and clearly appeared and acted as one of high social standing. Hall's manner of speaking the language gave away what many believed to be close connections to the Royal Family—his slender body, a stiff upper lip, and easy graceful ballet-like movements gave credence to the origins he claimed. Dressed perfectly in the finest from Savile Row, his dark hair was slicked back. John Lobb would be proud of his shoes.

In a topsy-turvy chain of events in the decade following his arrival in the staid and sleepy seaport town, Hall became a darling of the downtown social set, had a sex change operation, married a black man, and claimed to have given birth to a daughter.

Events such as these might have gone largely unnoticed in a metropolis like New York City, Paris or London, but inattention to such events would most assuredly not be the situation in Charleston, South Carolina in the mid-20th century. Much of the notice given these shattering developments was spoken of in whispers in the confines of downtown houses in an attempt to hide them from those who viewed such things as cracks in the closely-guarded armor of Charleston's respectability. Despite all, there could be no denying that it was happening.

Soon after his arrival, Hall was lavishly entertained by many in the Holy City, a description by which the town is now widely known. Invitations flowed into his house on Society Street and his presence was sought in the grandest houses south of Broad Street—generally regarded as the core of upper-class society. His reception into the houses in the city's lower regions was a signal to others far and wide that he was an acceptable dinner guest. This, despite that the house he settled into was in Ansonborough, a recently-rehabilitated section covering several city square blocks extending four blocks north of Broad Street and from Meeting Street eastwardly to the harbor. A section of the Holy City that had been down at the heels since the days of the Civil War, Ansonborough was not a place to live in the estimation of those quiet folk South of Broad.

One of the most ardent sponsors of Hall's initiation into downtown social circles was an early leader and founder of one of the local historic preservation organizations. It was a venerable local institution that saved many old houses from destruction by developers looking for ways to spend money made in the wake of World War II, which included replacing old buildings with new ones.

Throughout recent history, preservation groups have been leaders in the wholesale rehabilitation of old buildings throughout the city and especially in Ansonborough. The revitalization of Ansonborough would be significant as one of the first examples in the nation of the restoration of the fabric of an entire 18th- and 19th-century neighborhood in one fell swoop. To lure an authentic and aristocratic English gentleman there was a real coup for a historic preservation group that was leading the charge. The notoriety also became Hall's ticket to immediate social prominence in a place where such status came neither quickly nor easily.

Taking full advantage of the circumstances that created his new status, Gordon Langley Hall made his way from one elegant dinner party to another all over South of Broad. He sometimes even deigned to accept an invitation to social functions in Ansonborough. News quickly spread in the town that Hall was also an author of some note, adding to his allure in a part of the country once described by H. L. Mencken as "the Sahara of the Bozarts."

Hall had left England in the early 1950s to accept a job as a newspaper journalist and editor in Canada. He then drifted south to a small town in Missouri where he wrote the society column for the town's local newspaper, the *Nevada Daily Mail*. One of his early books, published in 1955, about his experiences in Canada before arriving in the United States, was entitled *Me Papoose Sitter*.

Along the way, Hall wrote several well-received biographies of people like Jackie Kennedy, Princess Margaret, and Mary Todd Lincoln. Basking in his prominence as an up and coming writer, Hall appeared in New York City in the mid-to-late fifties. It was there that he was befriended by Isabel Lydia Whitney, a prominent New Yorker he claimed as his cousin. Gordon told his friends that he and Isabel were cousins through the Harris-Cummings line of Isabel's family. Miss Whitney and her recently-deceased sister, Hasseltine Whitney, lived at 12 West 10th Street in Greenwich Village.

A descendant of Eli Whitney, inventor of the cotton gin, Miss Whitney was a watercolorist and an illustrator of children's books. She was well known for painting frescoes all over America in the early 20rh century, a career cut short only by an accident in her New York apartment in the mid-1920s when she fell in her kitchen. It was there, after Hasseltine's death in the early '50s, that Gordon was given an apartment on the fourth floor to live in and pursue his writing career.

During his sojourn at the 10th Street house, Gordon described some interesting events and happenings in a Memorial Exhibition program. Some of Isabel's paintings were displayed after her death at a neighborhood gallery which, in 1962, she had founded and named "Pen and Brush" at 16 East 10th Street. Gordon wrote in the program that before he and Isabel prepared for the exhibition, they had been visited by the likes of The Archbishops of both Canterbury and York, H.R.H. Princess Ileana of Romania, a great-great-granddaughter of Queen Victoria, Pearl Buck, Margaret Rutherford, and, on one occasion, 15 Anglican bishops in town for a meeting.

He said he and Isabel had received a personal message from Queen Elizabeth II upon her coronation in 1953, thanking them for putting on a pageant portraying the lives of the kings and queens of England in honor of the occasion at St. Martin's Church in lower Manhattan. The painting exhibition program further described the installation of a 14th-century monastery bell, bearing the arms of Medici. The bell was in the courtyard of the 10th Street house that was dedicated in 1955. Isabel rang the bell every July 4th and on the Queen's birthday.

Gordon's first trip to the South occurred in 1961, when he visited New Orleans and Charleston, looking for a place for him and Isabel to spend the winter months. It was in Charleston that he found a suitable house at 56 Society Street.

Reporting his find to Isabel, Gordon contacted the preservationists about buying the house soon after his return to New York. The Charleston preservationists leaped at the opportunity to enhance the credibility of the neighborhood project by showcasing Isabel and Gordon in one of the derelict houses. A representative of the group was promptly dispatched to New York with a proposed contract to present to Ms. Whitney and Gordon to cement the transaction.

The structure was a typical Charleston single house, reflecting what was said to be the prevalent English Barbadian architectural style in the city. Set with the front door opening down a few steps to the sidewalk, perpendicular to the street, and one room deep, the house had a driveway along its side and a small garden and carriage house in the rear. One of the special attractions of the property was a beautiful large live oak tree in the side yard. Miss Whitney, anxious to please her friend and protégé, purchased the house right away, and she and Gordon began making plans for the needed restoration.

Isabel unfortunately died on February 2, 1962, before Gordon had begun any of the work to restore the Charleston house. He took her body to old Heathfield in England for burial at All Saints Church on the feast day of Saint Valentine. After the funeral, Gordon returned to Charleston and began the restorative work on the Society Street house, fulfilling what he said was Isabel's dream. In her will, she left Gordon the 10th Street house in New York and its furnishings, the Society Street house in Charleston, $2 million earmarked for the restoration of the Charleston house, and an additional amount to fund Gordon's desired lifestyle in his new home. He took up permanent residence in the Charleston house on September 2, 1962.

Gordon's acceptance in the town's highest social circles was immediate. Many of the South of Broad residents who encountered him at social gatherings saw him as a sort of modern-day British immigrant. He quickly became a darling of the cocktail and dinner party circuit. It was clear to those of the preservation effort that he would add to the authenticity of the period they desired to emulate — colonial America in the Lowcountry as it had been in the 17th and 18th centuries.

Gordon's background was not at all what they had been led to believe. His mother was Marjorie Hall Ticehurst, whom Gordon described as a British aristocrat of Heathfield, Sussex, England. His father, Jack Copper, was a chauffeur at Sissinghurst, the Nicolson house in Kent. Gordon was their illegitimate son.

In *Dawn: A Charleston Legend*, an autobiography Hall later wrote under the name Dawn Langley Simmons, he says he was born in 1937. But news reports at the time of his death gave his birth year as 1923. The latter is likely closer to the truth, as he had been a well-established author in Canada and America before 1955.

Gordon first met Margaret Rutherford, the famed English actress, when she and her husband, Stringer Davis, arrived in New York in 1960. She came to play a role in the play "Farewell, Farewell, Eugene." It was during this short visit to the city (the play closed after only seven performances) that she and Gordon first met when she visited him and Isabel at home. It was the beginning of a long and interesting relationship.

Dame Margaret later described her visit in New York with Gordon and Isabel this way: "They both could have stepped out of a play, Miss Whitney ageless and gracious with her bluish-gray hair piled upon her head rather like Queen Mary's...She walked with a light aluminum crutch which she manipulated with the dexterity of a nubile mountain goat." She described Gordon as "...dark-haired, high cheek-boned and frail. Gordon's large brown eyes, inherited from some long-dead Andalusian ancestor," she said, "haunted me all through that evening's performance. He sat with a large green and red Amazon parrot named Marilyn on his shoulder who had just been photographed for *Life* magazine." It was a few days later that Gordon, then claiming to be 23 years of age, says that Dame Margaret insisted that he become her and Stringer's adopted child and become a part of their family. After this alleged encounter, Gordon referred to her as "Mother Rutherford."

Josephine Humphreys, a modern-day Charleston author who lived for some years in the house at 56 Society Street after Gordon's time there, wrote a piece in 1989 for *The New York Times Magazine* that sets the scene for what happened next in the story of the life of Gordon Langley Hall in the Holy City.

"My house," she wrote, "was built in 1838 by a writer-historian, a Unionist who wrote *Traditions and Reminiscences of the American Revolution, Chiefly in the South*. Of equal interest to me is a more recent owner, a writer-historian-transsexual who restored the house during the 1960s; she wrote *Man Into Woman*. In my yard is a freestanding piece of brick wall with a window in it, relic of a burned kitchen-house dating from 1750, and an elaborate pet cemetery with little statues, dating from 1965. That's a rich history, I figure. Complicated and mysterious."

Beginning in 1964, when Gordon returned from a trip to England, the circumstances of his sexual identity became the issue of the day in Charleston. Word about it began to creep out...but many in the downtown precincts tried to keep it off the streets and behind the walls of the houses. Dawn, the name she assumed after the sex-change operations, wrote in her autobiography that Gordon experienced menstrual bleeding sometime before 1968, a fact he said was confirmed by a Charleston physician. That development, he told the people in the Holy City and others, led to his conclusion that he had always been a woman, and only a little surgery was needed to make the fact meet the reality of the discovery. The autobiography reports that after the sex-change surgery, her breasts began to grow, and other aspects of her physical feminine nature rapidly developed.

While the sex-change project was underway, Gordon spent time at the White House gathering material to write a biography of Lady Bird Johnson who, with her husband Lyndon B. Johnson, was then the occupant of the place. On one of his visits to see the Johnsons, Hall took one of his Charleston dogs—an old chihuahua named Richard-Rufus that had, he said, been given to him by a Charleston veterinarian. A highlight of the visit was what Gordon described the "thrill and delight" that the President enjoyed bouncing Richard-Rufus on his knees.

But a big concern Gordon felt during the White House visit was self-consciousness about his sexual appearance, and the worry that the security personnel would be suspicious that he was attempting to hide objects under his clothing because, he said, his breasts were swelling and the jacket he was wearing did not hang right. Despite all the worry, his enlarged breasts did not cause alarm, the visit was enjoyable, and the work on the biography proceeded as planned.

The large number of animals that Gordon kept at the Society Street house and the amount of care they required led to a significant professional relationship with the veterinarian. Gordon was probably the vet's largest account, but their relationship soon soured when he could no longer pay the mounting bills. Without Isabel's money and the diversion of funds to cover the costs of his sex-change surgery, he was producing much less income from writing projects. Serious financial problems soon appeared on the horizon.

Gordon's first of many encounters with the local judicial system came when his veterinarian retained a prominent local law firm to help him collect the money owed for the treatment of the animals. Members of the law firm had heard of Gordon's big splash in the town's social circles, but the lawyers were not high enough on the social grid to have been a part of his extravagant welcome.

By today's standards, the amount Gordon owed the vet was not large, but in the 1960s, it was a substantial sum. Gentle requests for payment were ignored, so a young lawyer in the firm, Langdon Gibbons—anxious to please superiors in the law firm and his clients— fired the first shot by filing a lawsuit in the Charleston County Court to collect the money. A defense to the claim on Gordon's behalf was immediately mounted by a prominent lawyer with close connections to the preservationist group that had acquired the Society Street house for Isabel and Gordon.

As the vet's cause inched its way toward a trial before the Honorable Theodore DuBose Stoney, the judge of the County Court, and son of a former mayor of Charleston, anyone aware of the latest downtown news sensed that the cards of the social establishment Gordon had graced had been called in and were being laid out on the field of justice. It seemed that those cards were stacked against the vet, but Gibbons persisted on his behalf.

As the date for the trial approached, Gibbons was in the judge's chambers trying to get the case scheduled for a hearing. Another prominent downtown lawyer, William McGillivray Morrison, Jr., was also there, likely as a curious bystander to watch the matter unfold.

Morrison, happily adding some spice to the proceeding, began regaling those sitting around the judge's chambers with stories of encounters he had had with Gordon during recent social events below Broad Street. Known as "Bo" to all who knew him, Morrison was also the son of a former mayor. He told the half-dozen or so lawyers sitting around in the room that he had been seated across the table from Gordon at a recent dinner given in his honor by a leading Charleston businessman and his wife.

The described dinner hosts were part of an old-line Charleston family of Huguenot descent. But they were among the first "below Broad Street" people who surprised all their neighbors and decided to settle in Ansonborough, just around the corner from Gordon's Society Street house.

Bo Morrison told the Courthouse gathering that Gordon had been the hit of the party. As the news of the party spread, invited guests from all over the city flocked to the social venues to see the new Englishman in town. He was the talk of the town, Morrison said, and it was almost as if Gordon was on display in a zoo.

He told the assembled group that there was a feeling among those at the Ansonborough table that old Charleston was finally waking up at long last to establish important lines of connection to its English roots, and that Gordon Langley Hall was their conduit.

The only disquieting aspect of the evening, Bo continued, had been Gordon's persistent reference to him as Beauregard, something that he had not encountered before this occasion. Clearly an allusion to an assumed connection between Bo and General Pierre Gustave Toutant-Beauregard, the Confederate Civil War general of New Orleans who spent a lot of time bombarding Fort Sumter. Even now, for good or bad, Bo is still called Beauregard by many in the city, and he happily answers to it.

Despite the anxiety about upsetting the downtown social set that Langdon and others in his law firm felt, the case against Gordon took its normal and just course. When all the cards were down on the table, it was decided by Gordon's advisors that a court appearance was beneath his dignity. His lawyer withdrew from the field and took Gordon with him, and the court awarded a judgment to the veterinarian for the amount of the outstanding bills.

None of the veterinarian's bills was ever paid. But more shocking developments came to the sleepy community as Gordon's assets were rapidly depleted and his life began changing in unimaginable ways.

A time came in the progress of Gordon's sex change when Langdon Gibbons, serving in a part-time position as a municipal judge of the City of Charleston, received a telephone call from Brantly Seymour, a Charleston lawyer. Seymour announced that he represented Gordon Langley Hall and that he was calling on Municipal Court business.

The problem, Seymour explained, was that Gordon was in the process of becoming a woman, but was not quite there, and that he was greatly concerned that the police might arrest him. He reminded the judge that the local laws prohibited a man from dressing and appearing in public as a woman. The purpose of the call, he said, was to inform the local judiciary that such a situation existed in the town, and to ask the judge to advise the city police of the situation. Gordon's lawyer contended that the transitional circumstances of Gordon's sex change should be an exception to the enforcement of the city ordinance, and wanted a ruling from the Court to that effect.

The judge informed Mr. Seymour that the Municipal Court was not able to give him an advisory opinion on the efficacy of the city ordinance in these unusual circumstances, but that if an arrest was made, he should inform the Court, which would have to then address the issue in a public proceeding. He further suggested to the lawyer that he should consider discussing the matter with the city attorney, Morris D. Rosen, since it would be he who would bear the responsibility for prosecuting any charges along these lines.

As it turned out, Gordon was not arrested for dressing as a woman, his sex change process continued to evolve, and the city was abuzz, as the scene on Society Street became stranger and stranger.

As the physiology of the sex change issues was being sorted out, Gordon legally changed his name to Dawn Pepita Langley Hall and, using the new name, was baptized at an African Methodist Episcopal Church on Smith Street in Charleston.

Hall explained it this way: The adoption of the name Dawn was an allusion to the dawn of a new day, as indeed it was for both

Gordon and Charleston society. The choice of Pepita as a middle name was for the grandmother of Vita Sackville-West of Sissinghurst, where Gordon's biological father was a chauffeur. Pepita, a Spanish dancer, was the mother of Victoria West through a liaison with Lionel Sackville-West, Vita's grandfather.

As if the sensation of the sex change was not enough to keep the town at rapt attention, there was another highly-charged jolt when word leaked out that Dawn was making marriage plans. The prospective bridegroom, John Paul Simmons, was a 20-year-old African-American automobile body shop worker and sometime shrimp boat hand.

The circumstance engendered just about all the reactions one can imagine. This time, emerging from the parlors of the stately homes into the streets, tongues were wagging all over town, some deploring the shocking news, some secretly savoring the scandalous gossip, while others experienced and expressed downright amusement.

Margaret Rutherford's reaction to the announcement of the marriage plan was widely reported. "I am delighted that Gordon has become a woman, and I am delighted that Dawn is to marry a man of another race, and I am delighted that Dawn is to marry a man of a lower station, but I understand the man is a Baptist!"

Some Charleston locals reveled in the tidbits of cascading news. The regulars at the back bar of the Carolina Yacht Club, an exclusive downtown men's club on East Bay Street, were heard to say that it was a pity that Dawn's expectations had dropped so low that she had to settle for a two-"m" Simmons rather than a one-"m" Simons (which was thought to be more acceptable), alluding to the local belief that the spelling of the Huguenot name Simon was somehow degraded by the use of two of the consonants.

Excitement and apprehension reached higher levels on a daily basis as the time of the wedding approached. A bomb threat on the eve of the wedding caused the ceremony venue to be moved from a church in another part of town to Dawn's house at 56 Society Street.

As the ceremony was about to begin, as an introit, "The Battle Hymn of the Republic" was played and amplified electronically while the bride approached the makeshift altar set up inside the house.

With the exception of Jack Leland, a reporter for a Charleston newspaper, news media representatives were not allowed to attend the ceremony. Leland's report of the events was published on the obituary page of the next day's edition of *The News and Courier*. Other journalists, including television reporters, waited outside in front of the house while the wedding was being solemnized inside.

Bernard Fielding, a local African-American lawyer representing the bridegroom was slated to give the bride away, but got cold feet at the last minute and left the house before the ceremony began. In *Dawn, a Charleston Legend*, she wrote that Mr. Fielding "at the last moment developed political ambitions and left me standing alone at the top of the stairs."

As he departed the premises, Mr. Fielding was stopped by a local television news reporter on the front steps of the house. When asked what was happening inside, sighing in obvious discomfort and nervously wringing his hands in front of the cameras, Mr. Fielding responded to the viewing public, "I don't know what's happening inside, but I'm gettin' outta here because I think this whole thing's gonna backfire."

Joe Trott, a florist, whose shop was nearby, was invited and attended because he provided the floral arrangements for the occasion. He reported that he thought the only safe place to sit or stand in the house was away from the Society Street windows because of the possibility of gunshots being fired into the house by passersby. Fortunately, the ceremony went off without bloodshed.

After the wedding, Dawn and her new husband John Paul left immediately for England so the bridegroom could be properly introduced to English society. Their activities soon after arrival in London, according to Dawn, included an afternoon tea with the Archbishop of Canterbury, The Most Reverend and Right Honorable Geoffrey Francis Fisher, which was arranged by Mother Rutherford.

Not long after the couple returned to Charleston, a daughter, Natasha, came into their lives. Dawn insisted to the end that the child's birth was natural and that she had a birth certificate to prove it. It became a common occurrence for her to be seen pushing a carriage with Natasha inside just across the street from the Mills House Hotel, headed to Society Street. It was only apropos that the area was essentially the same place where the Secession Convention had been held in 1860, and the lawyer James Louis Petigru opined that South Carolina was "too small to be a republic and too large to be a lunatic asylum." And so it goes...

Almost as soon as the reality of the new arrangement began to settle in Charleston, the lives of Dawn and John Paul headed steadily downhill, sadly and tragically leading to one serious setback after another for the couple. Dawn soon became an outcast in the city; the Society Street house was lost to foreclosure, and John Paul became the victim of a serious mental illness and died in a mental institution in New York. Dawn left Charleston and died in a town in upstate New York.

Even so, Gordon Langley Hall would not be soon forgotten by those who knew him.

THREE
AN ENGLISH VISITOR

The South Carolina Historical Society sent a notice to all its members in the fall of 1999 announcing that it was hosting a black tie event on October 24th at Charles Towne Landing, site of the original colony. All the Society members in Charleston and around the state received the fancy invitation to celebrate the publication of a new edition of the Shaftesbury Papers and to hear an address given by Anthony Ashley Cooper, the Earl of Shaftesbury. The Earl would be autographing copies of the Papers for all in attendance at the dinner, and the governor of South Carolina would be there to introduce His Lordship.

The Shaftesbury Papers are a collection of documents in a volume first published by the Society in 1897. It is a valuable collection of papers concerning the plan for the settlement of Carolina formulated by Anthony Ashley Cooper and the other Lords Proprietors. Five hundred sixty bundles of documents in the collection relate to a variety of family business issues. Bundle 48 contains the papers related to the founding of Carolina—including those created by John Locke that pertain to the structure of colonial governance by the Lords Proprietors. Transcripts of the documents in Bundle 48 were obtained by the City of Charleston in 1883, and later came into the possession of The South Carolina Historical Society. Langdon Cheves, a member of the Society and a notable local historian, edited the documents, and the Society printed 500 copies.

Anthony Ashley Cooper's name is more recognizable in the modern Lowcountry world than those of his fellow colonizers. First of all, the two rivers that make the City of Charleston a peninsula bear the names Ashley and Cooper and are used by many public and commercial institutions nearby.

There is an Ashley Hall School, an Ashley Avenue, an Ashley Dental Associates, Ashley Liquors, an Ashley River Ob/Gyn Clinic, and many more. Not to be outdone, there is a Cooper Hall Senior Assisted Living Community, a Cooper River Baptist Church, and so on.

In recent years, ads began to appear for a new real estate development to be called Ashley River Club, proclaiming the following: "Anthony Ashley Cooper would be proud. It produces one of the most revolutionary building systems in home construction today: Noise elimination, Wi-Fi throughout, exceptional vapor barrier, purified air and water systems, resistance to all types of weather."

And the granddaddy of all the Coopers in the Lowcountry is the newest bridge over the Cooper River, a 2005 architectural masterpiece that links the peninsula of Charleston with the Town of Mount Pleasant.

The new span was named to honor Arthur Ravenel, Jr., a local politician who helped raise the money to fund its construction, and whose forebears came to the Lowcountry with the first wave of Huguenots that Ashley Cooper and his colleagues arranged in 1680 to swell the population of the colony.

The Ashleys and Ashley Coopers have made Wimborne St. Giles in Dorset, England, their home since the 15th century, but the title Earl of Shaftesbury began with Anthony, bestowed on him soon after the 1670 settlement of Carolina. The prominence he acquired from his Lowcountry business success and his leadership in colonial development has made the Ashley Coopers a leading family of the English realm ever since.

Indeed, Anthony Ashley Cooper's organizational and business acumen made the first settlement at Charles Towne Landing in 1670 a success that endures to this day, over 300 years later. It was his imagination and foresight that led him to commission the creation of a framework for the colonial government by John Locke, the noted English philosopher who wrote the Fundamental Constitutions of Carolina. It was due to his planning and persistence that the lines of supply and communication to the new colony remained in place to nourish and assure the survival of the people who settled the new land. It can be argued that Lord Shaftesbury, above all others, was responsible for the viability of the Carolina colony.

To ensure continued involvement by the founders, the development company organized by the Lords Proprietors—and led by the earl—set aside grants of substantial tracts of land for each of them. Shaftesbury's portion was on the west bank of the Ashley River near the site of the first settlement.

More than any of the other Lords Proprietors, the descendants of Anthony Ashley Cooper have maintained a continuing connection to the former colony. Throughout successive generations, they have followed the progress of the descendants of those first settlers they planted in the Lowcountry. For example, the 10th Earl of Shaftesbury, also named Anthony Ashley Cooper came to Charleston in 1967 to participate in planning the 300th anniversary of the city's founding.

It was, therefore, not a surprise for Charleston community leaders to learn that the earl would return in the fall of 1999, after an absence of more than 20 years, to commemorate the publication of a new edition of the Shaftesbury Papers under the auspices of The South Carolina Historical Society.

On a day in late September, just after the Society invitations were mailed, Langdon Gibbons, a lawyer and member of the Society who lived in the heart of downtown, walked home from his office—a distance of about two city blocks—for the midday meal. In Lowcountry parlance, that midday meal is called "dinner," the traditional name given to the meal between breakfast and supper by many of the locals living on the Lower Peninsula.

Dinner at midday is an institution still carried on as an act of peaceful defiance by a now small band of Charlestonians who refuse to acknowledge the dawn of the 20th century or any modern conveniences, including the advent of air conditioning in the South. A tradition that many city dwellers in the Lower Peninsula acquired at birth, it will endure as a part of their everyday life until they die, and will likely be carried on by their descendants as long as the sun shines on the land.

The tradition is a holdover from the days when the only way to escape the blazing heat in summertime was to slowly walk home for a mid-afternoon meal at 2:00 or 3:00, and then, after the discovery of electricity, take a nap in the breeze of an attic fan that pulled warm air throughout the whole house. After completion of the nap, one would stroll back to one's office at around 5 o'clock to finish up the work of the day by 8 p.m.

The workday ended with another slow walk home at dusk for "supper." Despite a cool fall and winter climate, and the introduction of Daylight Savings Time, the routine set by this tradition carried through all the year long without seasonal variance.

Langdon's is a typical Charleston single house with architectural features that the locals say was inspired by the early Barbadian settlers. Called single houses because they are rectangular in shape and generally only a single room wide, they were constructed to take advantage of the prevailing breezes from the southwest in minimizing the effects of the stifling summer heat.

Most of the single houses are set on their lots so that one of the narrow sides of the rectangle is flush on the lot line at the front, usually at the edge of the sidewalk. The wooden ones are plentiful because of the availability of good heart pine and cypress from which they were made.

There are also many houses on the peninsula that are made of English bricks that were brought as ballast on ships in the heyday of English colonial shipping to the port in Charleston. They are usually three stories with porches or piazzas on one of the long sides of the rectangle running the length of all three floors.

The entrance to the single houses is through a door that opens onto the first-floor porch directly from the sidewalk, and then there is, more often than not, another entrance door about halfway down the length of the house. This door leads into an entrance hall with a living room on the left side of the hall and a dining room on the right.

Modern single houses have been designed, and the old ones modified, to accommodate modern conveniences such as bathrooms, air conditioning, and inside kitchens, features that did not exist in the original structures. There was no air conditioning in the Lowcountry until after World War II and, in earlier days, the bathrooms were originally privies in the yards. The kitchens were usually in separate buildings behind the houses.

In the neighborhood is a much grander house built and lived in by Gibbons's fifth-great-grandfather, John Rutledge, who was a principal drafter of the United States Constitution and appointed by George Washington as the second Chief Justice of the United States. Directly across from the John Rutledge house is that of his brother Edward, who signed the Declaration of Independence. On the east side is a house that once belonged to another Rutledge brother, Hugh, who served as Chief Justice on the South Carolina Supreme Court.

Arriving for "dinner" on this particular late September day, Langdon picked up the mail from the box on the back of the street door, and stepped up onto the first-floor porch leading to the main entrance of his house. He found his wife Colette in the kitchen, which had been added on at the rear of the original structure, giving final directions to Beulah and Lizzie, a mother-and-daughter team who performed the housecleaning and the midday cooking. (Lizzie was the third generation of her family to work in the house. Her grandmother, Mary Washington, served the family before when the children were growing up.)

Langdon and Colette had been married for ten years. Between them, the two had three children, all grown and living in homes of their own. In his usual fashion, Langdon sorted the mail, putting Colette's in one pile and his in another. One envelope—the invitation to the Society dinner—was addressed to both of them.

He showed it to Colette, who looked at the invitation with a quizzical eye. "I wonder if that's the same Tony Shaftesbury I used to know," she said.

Colette had been born and grown up in the countryside on a farm near Grasse in the South of France. In European style, her parents had provided her with a classical education, and she'd attended schools in France, England, and Belgium. This, to round out her exposure to all the things a European woman needed to know and to help her succeed in circles of similar people she would meet all over the world.

Colette explained to Langdon that before their marriage, she had been an avid participant in shooting parties in Europe— pheasant shoots in England and France and red-legged partridge shoots in Spain—which were attended by the likes of the Earl of Shaftesbury and other European noblemen. Grand country affairs that went on for days, the shooting parties brought out the women in their best sporting finery, the men in their tweed jackets and ties, and pairs of the finest Purdey and Holland and Holland shotguns the world had to offer. The days of these parties, she said, were planned around the shooting of birds in the mornings and afternoons, elegant noontime luncheons in the field, and convivial evening dinners on the estates.

Colette reported to Langdon that some of the most elegant shoots she attended were hosted by Tony Shaftesbury at Wimborne St. Giles. There she'd met Bianca Le Vein, a charming Italian-born woman 12 years the earl's senior, who was then the Countess of Shaftesbury.

It took Colette only one phone call to a mutual acquaintance to confirm that her old friend Tony was indeed the same Earl of Shaftesbury soon coming to Charleston to speak at the dinner. So, without further thought about it, she asked Langdon to order the tickets and he did.

October 24th, a Sunday, was a pleasant Lowcountry day. The feel of fall was in the air, and the leaves on the trees were showing the first signs of the seasonal change that comes with cooler temperatures. Langdon and Colette, who were hosting a luncheon for friends, were on their way home from morning services.

His Lordship's visit to the city had been reported in the local newspaper, and it was from his photograph in the article that Langdon recognized Shaftesbury crossing King Street at the corner of Broad. When he pointed the gentleman out to Colette, she quickly hopped out of the car to greet him—and a beautiful young woman walking with him.

The earl told Colette that he and his companion, Sophie, had been walking around South of Broad looking for a house to buy. Colette immediately asked them to come to their house, and the couple readily accepted the invitation. The three of them walked the short distance to the house while Langdon parked the car.

When they were all collected inside, Langdon asked Shaftesbury if he would like a glass of champagne. His Lordship immediately responded, "I have never refused one." The response became familiar during the course of the day.

A man of average physical stature and typical British upper-class confidence, His Lordship was the sort of person who was comfortable anywhere. He was naturally at ease, and really quite charming and engaging. Those in his presence felt a sense of impending adventure, and his natural charm put those around him in a comfortable frame of mind, ready to join whatever exciting opportunities for action might be presented.

Anthony Ashley Cooper, like all of his forebears, had been born in 1938, the son of a British father and his second wife, Françoise Soulier, a French woman. Tony's father had first been married to Sylvia Hawkes, a London chorus girl who, after their divorce, married Douglas Fairbanks and later, Clark Gable. His father died before inheriting the earldom, and upon the death of Tony's grandfather in 1961, Anthony succeeded to the title of the tenth Earl of Shaftesbury.

Tony's own first marriage was to the Italian Bianca Le Vien, whom Colette had met at the shooting parties. After ten years, the marriage ended without an heir, but the earl's second marriage in 1976—to Christina Casella, a Swedish woman—produced two sons.

During the course of the afternoon visit, Tony told Colette that he was now living in an old water mill that had been restored as a house beside a river near Bordeaux in southwestern France. He had turned over the family estate at Wimborne St. Giles to his two boys, he said, to prepare for the eldest son's accession to the earldom.

Sophie, the earl's companion, was a delightful young woman, perhaps a little less than half His Lordship's age. Tall, with dark hair, her mahogany-colored skin was soft and light, and she was properly and generously proportioned in every way. Attired in jeans and a tee shirt for the morning, her appearance belied the look of the poet she said she was. She lived, she told the Gibbons, in Montmartre, the artist colony on the north side of Paris.

Uncertain as to whether he had heard Sophie clearly, Langdon asked if it was Montmartre, the famous artist colony, or Montparnasse where she said she had lived in Paris. (Montparnasse was a part of the city where Benjamin Franklin had lived when there.) She said no, it was Montmartre, explaining that Montparnasse was a place in Paris where there were several very tall and ugly modern buildings. They were so ugly, she said, that some people lived in them only to avoid having to look at them from the outside. (As Sophie was not his idea of what a Parisian poet should look like, Langdon was not surprised later to learn that she had been born in New York and had grown up in Los Angeles.)

Sophie was equally at ease during the conversation. It became quickly apparent that she, too, would easily fit right into the plans for the day, whatever they turned out to be. After a glass or two of Verve Clicquot de Ponsardin, Langdon too felt quite comfortable. The prospect for enjoyment of the rest of the day was bright and on a sound footing.

Langdon poured more champagne into glasses around the room. After about an hour from the starting gun, he looked out of a living room window and saw the first luncheon guests approaching. Colette's sister Camille was walking toward the house with another person he recognized as an old friend of the sisters who had taken a break from his American tour of the Lowcountry to see them.

The number of people in the house began to swell just as the first bottle of champagne was headed toward its end, adding new and interesting prospects for the robust conversation already underway. The new arrivals, had not, of course, known the Earl and Sophie would be there, so there was an element of pleasant surprise as each new guest came into the house.

Langdon handed the champagne bottle to His Lordship to finish the rounds and hurriedly ran outside to explain the scene to Camille. The person with her was a Frenchman, Jean Paul d'Amblimont, who had spent the night before at Bonaventure, Camille's plantation in the southern part of the Lowcountry. Jean Paul, about the same age as His Lordship, lived at an ancestral home estate in the French countryside near Versailles.

The two European noblemen didn't know one another. Looks and glances passed between them as if two dogs were eyeing one another. Jean Paul and Colette were standing by themselves on one side of the living room when he leaned over to her and quietly asked who Tony was. She responded by saying, "The simplest way to explain it is to say that his family used to own South Carolina."

As Colette gave the other guests a tour around the house, His Lordship and Langdon sat in the living room sipping champagne and conversing about Charleston and its history, a subject that Shaftesbury was keenly interested in learning more about. During the conversation, he asked Langdon about how he and Colette spent the Lowcountry summers, which he knew were often hot, humid, and uncomfortable.

Langdon replied that they sometimes went to Europe for a while each summer, but that he, because of the demands of his law practice, now generally spent most of the summer there. He explained that his family's fortune had been greatly diminished by the events of the Civil War and that he was now one who had to work for a living. His Lordship responded with the speed of a bullet, saying, "It's unfortunate that the world has come to that, but I myself have had to work feverishly for the last year and a half settling my mother's estate."

Even more people drifted into the house and the champagne continued to flow. Colette arranged the table settings to include His Lordship and Sophie. The next arrival was William Meriwether Bowen, an old friend of Langdon's from his days in law school and in the Navy. He and Langdon had become good friends at the height of the Cold War when they served in highly secret naval operations, placing shore defenses along the Atlantic seaboard.

Bill and his wife, Caroline, were in Charleston attending to events around the birth of a new grandson. Bill, a person of uncanny judgment when it comes to assessing a situation on the ground, and perhaps sensing the need to address what he observed in strong terms, deferred from the offer of a glass of champagne, and asked for a generous portion of Beefeater gin (no vermouth, over a little ice with a twist of lemon).

For His Lordship, the champagne soon gave way to martinis, and then on to a pleasant *pouilly fuiseé* that Langdon had on hand. Caroline, detained by the new grandchild's birth, arrived after the luncheon began, completely unaware of any of the events that had now transpired over a couple of hours. She seemed to be in a sort of a quizzical daze. Compounding Caroline's confusion, Langdon seated her at the table between His Lordship and Jean Paul.

The conversation at the table was rich, interesting, and full, turning from reminiscences of the old shooting parties in England and Spain to his old school days at Eton and Christ Church Oxford, to stories about his regiment—which he said was the only unreconstituted regiment in Her Majesty's army—to descriptions of the land the Shaftesburys used to own in the Lowcountry and elsewhere in America.

During the first lull in the conversation, the Frenchman created his own little ceremony by presenting mementos to Collette and Camille—pretty little necklaces that he had brought with him to give to them as symbols of their long friendship.

As the sun began to dip in the western sky, those at the luncheon table continued the entertaining conversation. Unbeknownst to them, time for His Lordship's speech was nearing, and some of the staff of the Historical Society were frantically searching all over town for him.

Suddenly realizing the lateness of the hour, Shaftesbury and Sophie hurriedly departed for their hotel to change into their evening clothes, and there found the members of the Society staff pacing the floor of the hotel lobby. It was now so late that someone would be required to hold a lantern to lighten the pages of His Lordship's notes so he could deliver his speech.

Langdon and Colette arrived at Charlestowne Landing just as the talk began, and were perhaps the only ones in the crowd who wondered if he would make it through given the alcohol-laced warm-up activities of the afternoon.

The speech was rigid in its formality, touching on Shaftesbury family history relating to the development of the Carolina Colony and how the family had kept in touch with descendants of the first settlers, just as he was now doing, through the centuries that followed the founding.

He also remarked about the current debate in the House of Commons to change the structure of the House of Lords, a plan that would further diminish the influence of that historic house of Parliament—a development he naturally deplored.

When the speech ended, an elegant dinner followed that was attended by the governor of South Carolina and many local dignitaries. The dinner was served under a tent that had been pitched for the occasion on the site of the 1670 settlement near the Shaftesbury lands. When all was complete, the crowd dispersed, floating into the dark night, feeling a certain confidence and pride that all was right with the world, and they would continue to prosper on the strong foundation that had been laid by the wise colonial founders and their progeny.

His Lordship and Sophie left the Lowcountry and headed for Palm Beach, from where they sent postcards to the Gibbons and other friends in Charleston. After a stop at Palm Beach, they planned to visit friends in Barbados, one of the last British colonies remaining in the world.

Three months later, on Christmas Eve, Langdon was napping in the late afternoon, girding his body and soul for the upcoming midnight Mass, when the ring of the telephone suddenly awakened him. Colette answered it in the next room. It was Tony Shaftesbury, calling from the jeweler Van Cleef and Arpels in New York.

Tony told her that he was there having a glass of champagne and a cigarette, waiting for American Express to clear a $43,000 credit card charge for a diamond ring.

Colette asked if he was getting married, and he replied, "Yes, but not to Sophie." He went on to explain that the ring was for a woman named Antonia and that they indeed were going to get married.

"And," he continued, "I am calling you to say that I have booked the Russian Tea Room on Central Park South for New Year's Eve, and Antonia and I want you and Langdon to come to the party."

Colette declined the invitation, explaining that she and Langdon would be in Charleston for Christmas and in France for the New Year celebration. They never saw Tony again.

In mid-2005, Colette received a phone call from a mutual friend. This time the news was bad. Anthony Ashley Cooper, age 66, had been murdered on the evening of November 5, 2004, near Cannes in the South of France.

His death was not confirmed until months later on April 20, 2005. Colette raced through Internet websites for news of Tony's fate and discovered reports of the tragedy in many European newspapers.

The English authorities had become suspicious of foul play when His Lordship failed to return to the place he was living at Hove, near Brighton in England, on the Channel coast. His family informed the French police about his disappearance and they launched an investigation, but nothing was found until months later, his decomposed body was found hidden in a ravine near the French-German border.

His Lordship's newest wife of fewer than three years, Jamila M'Barek, age 37, was arrested, questioned, and later committed to a mental hospital in Nice where she was treated for extreme stress. The French Court at Grasse put her under official investigation for the murder of her husband, usually a prelude to criminal charges. Her brother, Mohammed M'Barek, age 40, was also arrested in Munich on suspicion of murder.

Jamila and Mohammed, who had been paid 105,000 pounds sterling by his sister to kill Tony, were tried in the Nice Criminal Court in May 2007 for the murder of Anthony Ashley Cooper, the 10th Earl of Shaftesbury. Both were convicted and sentenced to prison terms of 25 years. They claimed the slaying had been an accident.

In retrospect, it seems that a clear pattern of change was emerging in His Lordship's lifestyle at the time he spoke to The South Carolina Historical Society and in the days following in the fall and winter of 1999 a pattern that steadily intensified until his death. The culmination of the pattern was confirmed when the London Telegraph reported that Lord Shaftesbury's death "demonstrated the dangers of the possession of inherited wealth coupled with a weakness for women and champagne."

The news reports about Tony's death soon began to hit the Lowcountry. The scandalous information ignited anew an interest in the sordid tales that emerged following his last visit to Charleston.

Colette wondered if Sophie, the young woman Tony brought with him to Charleston, was really just another woman he had taken up with in 1999, when he'd visited the Lowcountry. Her curiosity was heightened when she read that Tony had "paraded" a young woman around Barbados in 1999. She, the newspaper reported, was a 29-year-old woman whom he met in a lingerie shop in Geneva.

Shaftesbury had introduced her to friends and curious news reporters as a member of the royal house of Savoy, but it was later revealed that she was really a French nude model and a Penthouse "Pet," with silicone-enhanced breasts. The revelation ended their relationship. His Lordship met Jamila the same year he was carrying on with Sophie, Antonia, and others.

The reports of Tony's bizarre behavior became stranger and stranger as time passed. There were reports of Viagra overdoses, testosterone injections, wild parties for which he dressed in circus-like costumes, and a steady parade of wild women.

The life of the 10th Earl of Shaftesbury began quite differently than the way it ended. He was given and received a splendid education, upheld the strongest civic values of his forebears serving as Chair of the Shaftesbury Society, and as chair of the London Philharmonic Orchestra for over a decade in the '60s and '70s, received the Duke of Cornwall Award for Forestry and Conservation in the early '90s, and was an officer of the British Butterfly Association.

But, as *The Daily Telegraph* reported on April 21, 2005, His Lordship was like Gladstone because it was thought that he had been helping vulnerable young girls working in nightspots on the French Riviera regain decent lives, but it now seemed that his involvement in such projects was born of more complicated motives. The depth and reality of the ignoble scenes that ended a long chapter in the story of the Lord Shaftesbury's life and death snugly fit into Aristotle's definition of tragedy as the "purification of a dangerous passion by a violent liberation."

Less than a month after Tony's body was found, *BBC News* reported that his son, Anthony Nils Christian Ashley Cooper, the *11th* Earl of Shaftesbury, age 27, had died suddenly in New York of an apparent heart attack. His brother, Nicholas Edmund Anthony Ashley Cooper assumed the title, and remains the 12th Earl of Shaftesbury. His son born in 2011 is in line to succeed him.

FOUR
THE REGIMENTAL SILVER

The origins of the American Revolution culminated in 1775 when colonists along the Atlantic coast began in earnest the long struggle toward independence from the mother country. The formal Declaration of Independence occurred the next year in Philadelphia when it was proclaimed by the political leaders of all the American colonies.

But the road to revolution and independence passed the point of no return before the declaration. South Carolina and the Carolina Lowcountry played a major role in the struggle as the fighting played out over the next several years. Some accounts show that more military engagements were fought in South Carolina than anywhere else in America. The British had thought it would be a short war and believed that a few troops could easily subdue the revolutionary upstarts. Instead, the war that developed was both long and hard and did not end until sometime in 1783.

As the months that began unfolding in 1775 turned into years, the British had the problem of keeping troops in the theater of operations at sufficient levels to prevail in battles that took place over wide geographical areas.

It was a difficult task indeed, as the British were accustomed to fighting wars in small land areas and mostly in Europe. Great battles were fought and won or lost in small fields as at Waterloo, Agincourt, Bosworth Field, or Tours.

British troops had not encountered guerilla warfare of the sort that would be presented to them by the rebellious colonists around the rivers and in the swamps of South Carolina. Nor did they expect that the colonists were united enough to prepare for life or death battles in all of the thirteen colonies from Massachusetts to Georgia, in Florida, and along the coast of the Gulf of Mexico.

By 1781, the British effort to subdue the revolution began to unravel. Their army had occupied Charleston since early 1780, an effort that had required Sir Henry Clinton and 11,000 men. By mid-1781 the only land in the colony they controlled was the Charleston peninsula.

Elsewhere in the colony, partisan bands led by Brigadier Generals Thomas Sumter, Francis Marion, and Andrew Pickens, and Continental Line forces led by General Nathaniel Greene successfully gained control of most of the territory. The rebel army routed the British and won over many of the Tories who remained loyal to the mother country. The handwriting began to appear plainly on the wall of resistance, revealing the sunrise of independence. Lord Cornwallis, the commanding British officer in the state, was pushed northward toward Yorktown. There he and his army met their fate in the battle that sealed the American victory in the War. It was at

Yorktown that the French army and navy led by the French General Rochambeau, Admiral de Grasse, and Lafayette, standing next to General Washington, sealed not only the victory over the British but also the eternal gratitude of the United States to France for helping to make independence a reality on these shores.

Thomas Sumter served early in the War, first as a captain in the 2nd Regiment, and then as a colonel, commanding the 6th Regiment of the Continental Line in South Carolina.

After the fall of Charleston, he withdrew from the fray for a variety of mostly political reasons and then was brought back into the struggle by what turned out to be an example of bad judgment by the British.

Cornet Banastre Tarleton and his legion visited Sumter's house in the High Hills of the Santee in the Backcountry. Sumter escaped as the British approached his house. The soldiers put Sumter's crippled wife, Mary Cantey Sumter, in a chair in the yard and set the house afire, forcing her to helplessly watch as her house burned to the ground. As legend has it, Tarleton's soldiers put a ham in her lap so she would not starve.

The enraged Sumter immediately accepted a commission as brigadier general in command of State Troops from Governor John Rutledge, a position he held for the remainder of the War. Sumter, with Marion and Pickens, led a furious assault not only on the British forces in the state but also against the Tories who had been a powerful force throughout the struggle in the Backcountry. Cornwallis, before his departure for Yorktown, labeled Sumter as his greatest plague in the Colonies.

The events in 1781 in South Carolina were discouraging for the British forces. They were meeting serious and determined resistance, and they controlled only Charleston. Their grip on it rapidly slipping, they were soon forced to withdraw from the pivotal southern city. They were short on troops and equipment and needed more men on the ground.

There were no military airlift squadrons or motorized supply lines in those days. Whatever they needed to defend them against the rebellion had to be brought with them or to them on sailing ships across the Atlantic Ocean.

Three British regiments comprising 2,200 men arrived in the port of Charleston in the summer of 1781 to try to regain a foothold and stem the rising tide of rebel resurgence. One of them, the 19th Regiment of Foot, known as the Green Howards, was commanded by Lieutenant Colonel James Coates.

The Green Howards arrived with 30 commissioned officers, 30 sergeants, and 672 infantrymen plus all the supporting cadres. It was divided into 10 companies, eight of which were designated battalion companies, and two of them were called flank companies. They arrived in the Port of Charleston on June 12, and its eight battalions of companies were immediately sent to man a garrison fortification at Moncks Corner, a Lowcountry town two miles west of the Cooper River and 35 miles north of the port city.

Two days later, on June 14th, the Green Howards at Moncks Corner were joined by about 150 members of a Tory band called the South Carolina Loyalist Calvary.

The two flank companies of the Green Howards were dispatched to relieve a fort under siege farther west at Ninety Six in the Carolina

Backcountry. Another new regiment, the 30th Regiment of Foot, was assigned to remain in Charleston to reinforce the occupying army. The 3rd Regiment of Foot was sent to a garrison in Orangeburg, a town 75 miles northwest of Charleston, to try to stem the growing strength of the rebels there. Thomas Sumter soon learned of the arrival of the Green Howards at Moncks Corner and the unfolding events led to his last hostile engagement of the War.

On June 16th, he sent a group of reconnaissance scouts to size up the situation and to try to get information about the Green Howards' plans. His scouts began by burning two boats that were tied up near the Wadboo Bridge and destroyed the bridge to prevent the easy movement by the regiment. The scouts were successful in the raid but were attacked and dispersed by the Loyalist Calvary.

Recognizing the presence of a significant rebel force commanded by the fiery Sumter, Lieutenant Colonel Coates decided it would be best to withdraw from the area to avoid a direct conflict with the soon-to-be Americans.

At 3 a.m. on April 17, the "Gamecock," the name by which Sumter was known to his troops, discovered that the 19th Regiment had departed Moncks Corner and was headed toward Charleston. Just after first light, Sumter and his men caught up with the enemy a few miles down the road at Huger's Bridge and pounced upon the rear guard of the Green Howards, which had become separated from the main force.

Along with the confiscation of the regimental supply wagons, sixty British soldiers were captured. The supply wagon booty included 720 guineas from the paymaster's chest, the books of the regimental library, and the regimental silver.

A battle ensued near Quinby Bridge and General Sumter, in a fit of fury for which he was known, made a violent charge toward the enemy. In his report of the engagement to General Greene, Sumter described the rifle fire from the British troops as "warm and close."

About a month later, the books that were taken from the regimental library were returned to the Green Howards, but the regiment never again saw the money or the silver that had been taken from them during the skirmish.

It was a brisk late October day in 1999. Langdon Gibbons was sitting at his desk in his Broad Street law office attending to routine matters. Among many phone calls from friends and clients that came in the late afternoon, was one from Bob Copperthwaite, a long-time friend from school days who now lived nearby.

Bob was a lawyer, but he was so embedded in scholarly pursuits that the practice of law took a second chair in his life. He devoted his time to matters he considered more important. Bob was an accomplished scholar of English literature and was also a student of the works of the Spanish writer Cervantes. His degrees were from schools in the United States, Canada, and England including such institutions as Sewanee, Princeton, and South Carolina in America, McGill in Canada, and Oxford in England.

Langdon first met Bob while they were undergraduates at Sewanee, near the beginning of Bob's long academic career. They often talked to one another and had been in close touch since the 1980s when Bob decided to embark on a career as a lawyer in Charleston. Their conversations covered a lot of issues through the years, but the incoming phone call was one of the strangest yet.

Bob began the conversation by telling Langdon about a visit he had recently made to York in northern England. He rambled quite a bit and seemed to be having a hard time getting to the point of the call.

Langdon, seated at his desk, trying to figure out how to meet some deadlines imposed by this or that lawsuit, was really distracted by the phone call. He fidgeted impatiently as Bob began spinning a long tale about visiting some army regiments in York, a subject about as far removed from anything on Langdon's mind as could be imagined. Bob droned on about how he had visited a military museum in Richmond, North Yorkshire, and had met there some people who were planning a visit to Charleston.

Langdon tried his best to be patient, consciously aware that Bob's normal voice in almost any conversation was sort of deadpan and his language was usually rambling. It was hard to understand what was really going on or in what direction the conversation was headed. After several minutes that seemed much longer, Langdon finally said, "Bob, what in the world is this about?

Bob, sensing Langdon's impatience, said, "I think you need to hear what I have to say. This could be serious business."

Langdon blurted, "What on earth are you talking about, Bob? What's so serious, and why are you telling me about it now? It sounds like just another one of those crazy situations you've gotten yourself involved in that leads to nothing but long conversations."

"No, Langdon, this doesn't involve me," Bob said. "It involves you!"

"Bob," Langdon shot back, "can we talk about this later"? I've got a lot of work to do. How about meeting me say at 5:30 in the Back Bar at Hibernian Hall?"

The Back Bar is a venerable Charleston institution where many members and guests spent the waning hours of workdays. Sometimes they're there until late into the night, and even into the early morning hours of the next day. Coming in from the outside the room, it's hard for them to see inside because the light in the bar is quite dim. The bar is on the right side of the room and there are four or five wooden top tables with four chairs each randomly placed throughout the room.

The air smells of three-day-old beer, and a dingy feeling is ingrained in the fabric of the walls that have been saturated by years of cigarette smoking. It's a place where for over 150 years all sorts and conditions of mankind have shared their ups and their downs with understanding comrades. It's a place where joyous events are celebrated, and where wounded souls go for sympathy and comfort.

But private conversations are difficult because the size of the room and the acoustics make what's meant to be a conversation at one table or at the bar one that eventually involves everyone in the room. This lack of privacy was no concern for Langdon, however, as he thought the whole thing was just another example of Bob's windmill tilting and some sort of a cynical joke.

Just as Langdon and Bob walked to the bar to order a drink, two men, Billy O'Hara and Mike Brennan—the only others in the room except for the bartender—sat down at a nearby table, each with a Guinness Stout in his hand.

Billy opened the conversation between the two with a simple question. "Mike, what's been going on in your life." The simple and short question was enough to start the flow of a sad tale of woe.

It began when Mike said, "It's been awful. My wife is having to undergo chemotherapy and radiation for her breast cancer. Her mother is in the hospital, had a stroke last week. A hurricane took the roof off the house, but it didn't matter much because the mortgage company had already filed a foreclosure on it. And I've got some sort of slipped disc that giving me a horrible backache. So, that's about how it is, Billy."

Using the affectionate southern family-like approach of a kind observer of adversity, Billy, in a dry monotone voice, responded, "Bubba, sounds like the wind done shiff on yo' ass!" The tone of the evening conversations was set.

Langdon and Bob took their Famous Grouse whiskey and sat two tables away from Billy and Mike. Langdon was hard pressed to hide his irritation. As soon as they sat down, he said:

"Bob, please explain to me what you've been trying to say about silver and some military museum you visited in England."

"Okay," Bob responded, "it's like this. I think I made a mistake. I was in England a couple of months ago, and I stopped by a military museum in York. It was in a town called Richmond. It's a museum of an old regiment, the 19th of Foot, called by the nickname the Green Howards. They're real proud of themselves because they say it's one of only two regiments in the British Army that has not been reconstituted since the days of the American Revolution. They seem to talk about that all the time."

Langdon impatiently interrupted, "What's the mistake, Bob?"

"I'll get to in a minute, but first let me tell you what they said."

"Said about what? For goodness sake, Bob, get to the point!"

"Just calm down, Langdon. I'm getting to it. Well, the officer in charge of the museum said that theirs was the only regiment in all of England that did not have its own regimental silver because it had been stolen. He said the regiment was in South Carolina, near Moncks Corner, in the summer of 1781, when General Sumter and a gang of partisan revolutionaries fell upon the Green Howards in a violent confrontation. Sumter, he said, not only took the silver but also took all their money and the regimental library. The library was returned three days later, but they've been looking high and low for the silver ever since. I told him I had an idea about where it might be. That was the mistake."

Langdon asked, "Where did you tell him that you thought it was?"

"I told him I thought you might have it!"

"You did what?" Langdon shouted. "Why in the hell would you say something like that, Bob? Incredible!"

"Well, Langdon, do you have it? I know there are some Sumters in your family background. Did it come down to you?"

"Do you mean, did the silver come down to me? I don't know. I'll have to look," he said, shaking his head in disbelief. "I might have some of it, but for god's sake, don't do anything to make this worse than you already have!"

Bob, adding fuel to a fire that was already hot said, "Langdon, it gets worse. They're coming to Charleston to look for themselves."

"When?"

"In mid-November."

"Who's coming?"

"The person who told me all of this is Major Donald Jones. He said his wife would be coming to Charleston with him. The major served on active duty for many years with the regiment, and runs the regimental museum in his retirement."

Langdon shook his head. "Well," he said slowly, "I guess I better look around and see if any of that silver is in the house or in the bank safety deposit box. I still don't understand why you dragged me into this thing. What made you think I might know anything about it?"

Bob was fidgety now, stammering a little, trying to figure out what to say next. He was beginning to feel that what began as an interesting playful diversion for him was getting a little bit out of control.

Bob, carefully choosing his words, said, "Langdon, maybe we should just tell the major that it was all a mistake, and there is really none of their silver here."

"No, Bob," Langdon said, "he's coming here and there will be a lot of questions about this silly thing. We just need to have some answers for him." He thought for a moment. "I guess I better tell Colette about it. She'll probably go ballistic. You know, we do have some of the Sumter silver, but I can't say that any of it is this English regimental silver you're talking about."

Langdon went home and explained the entire episode to Colette. As predicted, she went ballistic, but Langdon calmly persisted. He laid out his plan for defusing this unfortunate situation. In traditional Southern style, they would kill these foreign visitors with kindness and send them home happy that they did not find the regimental silver. There would be no silver in the house, and Langdon would explain what happened to it.

As a member of the Society of Colonial Wars, he and Colette would be attending the Society's Fall Court as its formal annual banquet is called. It is a hereditary organization that celebrates events of the American colonial era, especially events that occurred in the

French and Indian War—sometimes called the Cherokee War—in which the English forces in the American colonies sought to protect their positions against the French and insurgent Native Americans.

The Society members are descended from colonial civil and military officials. Langdon was eligible to be a member of the Society because of his descent from Thomas Sumter.

Langdon told Bob that he would invite Major Jones and his wife to attend the annual banquet of the Society of Colonial Wars. He asked Bob to extend the invitation and when he did, to find out the name of the major's wife so it could be put on a place card for the dinner that would be held at the Carolina Yacht Club in downtown Charleston.

Anticipating an acceptance of the invitation, Langdon told Colette to go and purchase sufficient champagne, Verve Clicquot de Ponsardin, at least three bottles, for pre-banquet aperitifs at their home, the scene of the search. He told her to hang the best portrait they had of General Sumter in the living room where the cocktails were to be served and to put it in the most prominent place so that nobody in the room would be able to miss seeing it. He told her to remove anything in the sideboards and closets that even remotely looked like English regimental silver, and to put it in their safety deposit box. And then told her to forget they had a safety deposit box.

As expected, Bob called with the news that Major and Edith Jones had enthusiastically accepted Langdon's invitation. The only thing left to be thought out now was an explanation of the whereabouts of the silver.

A few days before the event, Langdon took all of the family's English flatware, goblets, and julep cups, put them in cloth bags, and deposited them in the far reaches of the silver storage room. He replaced them with all the French silver pieces that Colette's family had given them, so that they, like the General's portrait, could not be missed.

The evening was cool and crisp, cool enough for Langdon to light a fire in the living room fireplace. The champagne was ready, and Colette had made some hors d'oeuvres of smoked salmon on small points of dark bread, a dish she had learned to make during her school time visits to Scandinavia.

The setting was elegant, so elegant, in fact, that Langdon thought it would be crude behavior for someone to bring up such an unpleasant subject as stealing. It would never happen in polite company, and he was sure that a major in such a distinguished British regiment would not stoop to it.

But Langdon wanted to end this silly charade once and for all. He decided to pick the right time and bring it up himself while they were having cocktails. He wanted the major to be able to look around the house to see for himself that the silver was nowhere to be found. He would take him on a tour of the downstairs of the house, and while they were in the dining room, he would tell the major the story of what happened to the regimental silver.

Major Jones and his wife arrived at the strike of six, along with two other couples who were also going to the banquet. The evening began softly and gently. The champagne, the steady glow of the fire in the darkened room, and the flicker of the candles that Colette put on the tables in the living room gave an irresistible glow to everything around, including the conversation.

In line with the plan he had set to deal with the issue of the silver, Langdon pointed to General Sumter's portrait and said, "Major, there's your man, the one who stole your regimental silver. Too bad it's not here anymore. I hope you haven't wasted a trip."

"No," the major crisply responded. "I really didn't expect to find it. I knew it would be a long shot, but was worth the effort to look around."

"Let me show you the rest of the house. Let's walk into the dining room."

The major and Langdon walked into the dining room. It was filled with pretty European furniture and more family portraits. Colette had arranged candles all around the room so that the soft rose-colored walls reflected a rich dim light.

The major commented on the beauty of the house, and the elegance of the French silver.

Langdon swiftly picked up on the compliment. "Yes, Major," he began, "I think I can help you solve the mystery of the regimental silver."

"Really," gasped the major.

"Yes," said Langdon. "That whole episode was well known in the legends handed down through the generations in our family. We also knew about the silver. I'm sorry to break the news to you, but you're 134 years too late to do anything about it.

"You see, some members of our family living in Summerville, just up the road, had the silver. At least, that's what my father told me. In the family, whose name was Brownfield, there were several unmarried sisters, great-granddaughters of General Sumter.

"Their parents inherited most of the general's household effects when he died in 1832 and there was talk through the years about English silver that had been a spoil of war. I'm pretty sure it was the silver you're looking for because they always called it the Green Howards silver."

"What happened to it?" exclaimed the major, now quite excited.

"Well, you see, Major, we had a visitor here in this part of the country in 1865 who caused us all a lot of trouble. We had a civil war going on.

"They heard he was coming because he started out in north Georgia, the state next to us, and headed to the sea, burning everything in his path. When he got down to Savannah, he headed our way.

"When the word got out, people packed up all their valuables and shipped them up to Columbia, a city in the center of the state. It seems that my great-great grandfather, General Sumter's grandson, went to Summerville when he heard that this man was coming toward us, gathered and took all his Brownfield cousins' valuable things to Columbia for safekeeping, the same as almost everyone else did."

Langdon looked down at the floor in mock shame. "Trouble is, he skipped us and headed straight to Columbia and burned it to the ground. Everything was lost, including your silver."

"Well," said the major. "I'm certainly sorry to get this news, but at least we know the answer now. I guess the mystery is solved."

Langdon, sinking into a relaxed attitude as the conversation with the major ended, said, "It's about time to go to the club. Let's get the wives together and head down there."

"Very well," said the major in sharp military diction, disguising the disappointment he felt at the news about the silver.

The four couples left the house for the short ride to the club that was just beyond a long stone's throw away. They arrived together and walked up the winding staircase to the ballroom where the dinner and dance would be held.

Langdon made arrangements with the Society's chief steward, Jonathan Lucas Yates, to set a special table for them in a prominent place to give Major and Mrs. Jones the feeling that they were honored guests.

The seating arrangement and the description of the history of the Society that was printed in the program for the evening. It told how the colonial warriors and the British were allies in the struggles that were being honored.

After putting their purses and other personal items on the table, the group circulated amongst the crowd that filled the room, stopping at the bar for wine or cocktails as they made their way across the ballroom floor.

Just before it was time to sit down for the dinner, Langdon asked the major to follow him to the head table to be introduced to the officers as an honored guest of the Society.

The governor was seated with his wife and other officers of the Society at a special table, beautifully decorated for the occasion. Prominent on the table were four beautiful silver Georgian candlesticks that stood out in their simple brilliance.

Langdon introduced the major and his wife to the governor, who stood up at his seat to greet them. As the major and Edith chatted away, Langdon's glanced at the candlesticks and froze. He suddenly remembered his grandfather's gift of old silver to the Society for occasions such as this. There, prominently engraved on the base of the candlestick, were the words:

His Majesty's Army
19th Regiment of Foot
North Yorkshire
1775

PART II

FIVE
SLAVERY

"This world is going to the dogs," he said. "It is being ruined by white men. We got along fine for years and years before the white men foisted their Negroes upon us. In the old days the old men sat in the shade and ate stewed deer's flesh and corn and talked of honor and grave affairs; now what do we do?"

~William Faulkner in *Red Leaves*

The great Southern paradox is that there is a rich and sweet culture in the Carolina Lowcountry that has grown out of the many generations of slavery—descendants of those brought from Barbados and Africa and from other English colonial settlements during the course of the development of the British colonial empire in North America. It is a paradox because the rich and wonderful culture of the region grew from a history of the worst oppression, involuntary servitude, and inhumane treatment of the African slaves at the hands of white slave masters that one can imagine.

The institution of slavery was formally introduced to the Lowcountry by the first settlers from Barbados, but the early Spanish explorers introduced the idea on the continent in the 16th century. They pressed Native Americans into involuntary service. Slavery was an established institution throughout the Caribbean when the

Barbadians, at the behest of the Lords Proprietors, settled Charles Towne in 1670. The developing New World colonization scheme included a plan for the introduction of slavery to provide labor for the agricultural products to be grown and, in the case of the Carolina colony, shipped mostly to England.

The purpose of imperial colonization was the development of natural resources to provide goods for trade and profit in the English world. There were few altruistic motives involved in the establishment of the Carolina colony by the British crown or by the Lords Proprietors who were chartered to develop the land.

It was a venture planned to make money for those who had been granted the charter. Human bondage became the prime means of producing goods for English markets at the lowest possible costs. Edward Ball writes in his book *Slaves in the Family* about the slaves of the Ball family in South Carolina and about his own descent from them, saying that the English became "the most efficient slave makers in history."

Leading up to becoming the most efficient slave makers in history was the development of the practice by humankind over an enormous stretch of time. It began as long ago as the birth of civilization when, at the genesis, humans inhabited the fertile crescent.

The socially acceptable and profitable practice of slavery among those who were slave owners expanded from its earliest beginnings to ancient Greece and Rome, and then to Europe in the Middle Ages. There was never anything about the institution that was comfortable, acceptable, or profitable for those human beings who were enslaved and oppressed.

Most sociologists agree that slavery still exists in America, but it is most often found in different settings and forms than in the early days of our history. Among the modern forms of it is the practice called human trafficking. Another form is the system of incarceration in jails and prisons in America. Many immigrants arriving in the United States from third world countries are consigned to slave labor despite federal laws prohibiting such practices. All this still exists in 21st century America.

There was nothing surprising or unusual about the standards of the English plans to establish a workforce of slaves in Carolina. Locke's *Fundamental Constitutions of Carolina* condoned the practice and set out the rules by which slavery would be conducted and governed.

The entire enterprise was organized and controlled from the mother country. At first, Carolina colonial slaves were brought by the settlers from Barbados and then, about 1700, English slave merchants began capturing them from the coast of Western Africa. They were imported directly to Charles Towne. Most of the early slaves were imported from Vy'est in Central Africa, and from as far north as Sierra Leone. A few of them came from the east coast and Madagascar.

The history of the slave trade from the 16th century until the end of it in the 19th century has been brilliantly documented by David Eltis and David Richardson in their *Atlas of the Transatlantic Slave Trade,* published in 2010 by the Yale University Press. A reader of this brilliant work discovers many important and interesting facts about the scope and magnitude of the Atlantic slave trade.

As an example, the numbers of slaves imported from Africa to North America from 1501 to 1867 (367,000) was dwarfed by those taken to Brazil (4,722,000). The numbers of slaves delivered to the islands of the Caribbean were also counted in the millions. A few of them, if 543,000 enslaved humans can be described as "a few," originated in Southeast Africa and Madagascar.

Although the British dominated the importation of slaves to North America, those numbers were dwarfed by the trade managed by other nations. In general terms, according to Eltis and Richardson, most of the slaves on British vessels were taken to the Caribbean and North America; the Spaniards took theirs to Puerto Rico and Cuba; the Portuguese to Brazil; the Dutch to the Dutch West Indies and Dutch Guianas; and the French to Sainte Domingue and other nearby French colonial islands. Others, in smaller numbers, were taken to the New World by vessels from Denmark, other Baltic States, and Germany.

When viewed in the overall context, the numbers are simply staggering. Even though the numbers of slaves brought to North America are relatively small compared to the overall importation to the Americas, those who were settled in the Carolina Colony have placed an indelible imprint on society throughout its history and have become a lasting influence on the rich Lowcountry culture that is unique and lasting in modern times.

As the Carolina slave population grew, the Lords Proprietors enacted a slave code in the early days of the colony that was the same as existed in Barbados. It was designed to define and control the slave population. The code left no doubt about the position of the slave in society: he or she was not a legal person but only a chattel, a piece of personal property, and the civil discipline of the human property was to be administered by the slave owner, not the government.

Offenses were defined, and written passes were issued to allow those enslaved to move around. Such documentation was issued by the owners to be held by the slave, and the passes were always required for movement outside the plantation or house of the slave owner.

The Carolina economy was at first supported by the production of such things as turpentine, rosin, and lumber, but soon after the colonial settlement took hold, the enormously profitable crops of rice and indigo began to take root, and both were later largely replaced by the labor-intensive production of cotton. The cultivation and marketing of rice and indigo made huge fortunes for the plantation owners, and South Carolina became, by far, the wealthiest colony of the original 13 North American colonies of Great Britain. Slave labor was the essential ingredient that made it possible to grow these crops.

The cultivation of rice and the great wealth of the white owners was made possible entirely by the knowledge, ingenuity, and enforced physical labor of the African slaves. Until now the contribution to the creation of our colony and nation by the African slaves has not been acknowledged by historians or by anyone else. Most agree that the time has now come in the 21st century for the recognition of this history.

The exploratory opening of the New World in the sixteenth century, principally by Portugal, Spain, and England, created an intense need for the development of slavery as an economic necessity. The Industrial Revolution was yet many generations in the future, and human labor was the only way to fuel the economic machines of the colonial developers.

Historians generally agree that over 40% of the slaves arriving in North America before the American Revolution came through the port of Charleston.

The flow of slaves through the so-called Middle Passage, the horrible voyage from the west coast of Africa to North America, more often than not led to Charleston. Lowcountry plantation owners soon developed preferences for the desired origin of the slaves they bought. It is said that the Charleston firm of Austin and Laurens, presided over by Henry Laurens, sought Gambians as the most preferred of the imports, and then those of the Windward Coast, and finally Angolans were believed to be the lowest quality of acceptable slaves.

As the agricultural economy grew, so did the slave population. The slave population of Charles Towne in 1708 was slightly larger than the white; but by 1720 in the farming areas of St. James, Goose Creek and St. James, Santee—both north of the city—the slave population exceeded 70% of the total population. By 1720, slaves outnumbered white people in the colony by more than two to one. In the early years, most of the slave population had been born in Africa, but by 1740, seventy years after the founding, they were almost all natives.

The slave population grew geometrically as ships filled with captive slaves continually arrived in the Lowcountry until the British government banned the importation of slaves in 1808. But generations of native-born slaves procreated and became well established early in the eighteenth century.

Growth of the African population in the Lowcountry was exponential. Most of the slaves worked on the plantations around Charleston, north to Georgetown and south to Beaufort. Many worked in the urban houses and shops of the masters, and some were taken to work on Backcountry plantations.

By the time of the American Revolution, there were over 75,000 slaves in the region. The numbers grew to 200,000 by 1810 as short staple cotton was introduced into the Carolina backcountry. By the time of the Civil War in 1860, the state's slave population exceeded 400,000. The availability of this low-cost labor reproduced itself as generations of new slaves were born and it led to Charleston's position as the wealthiest city in the North American colonies. Some of the Lowcountry plantation owners became the wealthiest men on the continent.

As the shackles of bondage began to loosen, however slowly, institutions came into being as centers of the African-American society. Slaves arrived on these shores without any knowledge of their ancestry or even their names.

The central social gathering was the church where they could meet and talk, both before and after emancipation. It was a place where they could share a common life. Slavery created a large segment of the colonial society that was void of hope in this life. The church was a natural centering point because it offered hope when there was no hope to be found anywhere else, and hope espoused in the churches centered on a longing for the life hereafter.

As a consequence, the church remains, in modem times, a focal point for the African-American community. There are not many successful politicians, black or white, in the Lowcountry who do not make regular rounds at African-American churches to try to solidify their constituent base to prepare for upcoming political elections.

In the eighteenth century, some southern slaves were able to obtain their freedom, and a number of freed slaves became slave owners themselves. This phenomenon led to the development of another class of citizens—free people who had been slaves.

In cities like Charleston, but especially in Charleston, groups like the Brown Fellowship Society were founded by freemen to provide decent burials for its members and their families, and to give the widows and children of deceased members a small stipend to cover some of their living expenses.

Membership requirements were that an applicant have brown skin and be of good character. Many of the Society members were men or descendants of men who had been born on nearby plantations and had been sired by white masters. In such circumstances, the white masters sometimes gave their own children their freedom.

Another layer in the Lowcountry social system has thusly grown from the slave plantation society that has enriched the whole culture. Saint Mark's Episcopal Church in Charleston is another example of an institution that was founded by brown freemen. Organized near the end of the Civil War, the church provided a place for former slaves and their descendants to congregate and socialize. It serves the same purpose in the twenty-first century. Recognized as a "black" church, some of its members, although entirely associated with the African-American community, have a skin color that is often indistinguishable from the whitest white person in the city. On the other hand, there are some "white" people now who were accepted into the most elite "white" social organizations such as Saint Philip's Church and the Saint Cecelia Society, whose ancestors came from the same mixed-blood plantation settings.

Social mores in the Lowcountry prevented and really prohibited a public recognition, much less a discussion, of this situation until late in the 20th century, when some of the history began to slowly seep out as racial divisions began to fall. Prominent brown members of the Lowcountry African-American community, some communicants of Saint Mark's Church, and some white people in the community have discovered that they share a common ancestry from the owners of the plantations, allowing them to now greet one another as blood relatives.

Some people who are not as secure as others about the truth of this situation have expressed the thought that "it is much too early in time to be bringing up such things" for public recognition. If not now, when?

The official end of slavery in the United States came on September 22, 1862 when President Abraham Lincoln abolished the institution by proclamation. However, neither the Emancipation Proclamation or the end of the great Civil War ended racial, economic, and social injustice. Oppression of the black minority continued unabated.

Millions of slaves were legally freed by the presidential proclamation, but little thought or action was taken to bring the former slave population into the constitutional life of the nation. Reform of laws and social institutions leading to justice for former slaves and their descendants has come about against political resistance from then until now.

The ill effects of slavery on the people subjected to it, and indeed on the entire population, cannot be measured and centuries will pass before the injustices wrought by it will be fully rectified—if such a state can ever be achieved.

In the mid-1980s, before the end of apartheid in South Africa, Desmond Tutu visited the United States, one of the first of many later visits to spread the voice of hope and justice. While attending a reception given in his honor in the nation's capital, he was asked what he thought could be done to solve the horribly complicated racial situation in his own country.

He shot back a response to the question, saying that the situation in South Africa was not complicated at all—that people were being oppressed and the oppression needed to stop. It was no more complicated than that.

The simplicity and power of his response cannot be avoided. The same is true in the Lowcountry and throughout America, both in history, presently, and in the future.

Slavery cannot be justified or glorified, and to try to romanticize it is to falsely present it. Nothing about it was just, glorious or romantic. It is most certainly a part of history, and that fact is inescapable and cannot be erased. But at the same time, it is undeniable that from the history of slavery has sprung a deep culture, laced with injustice, that has contributed to the richness of the character of the Lowcountry, and it is a part of its history that will never be disjoined.

The history and culture of slavery in the Lowcountry has contributed to a modem day transformation of politics and social justice in America. The ancestors of Michelle Obama, the wife of the 44th president of the United States, lived and worked as slaves on Friendfield Plantation near Georgetown, South Carolina. It is believed that Jim Robinson and his wife, Tenah, were her great-great-grandparents. Jim Robinson was born there in about 1850, and worked there, in slavery, in rice fields on the plantation. His master was a white man named Francis Withers who, like Michelle Obama, was educated at Harvard University.

It is likely that Jim Robinson's parents or grandparents were brought to Georgetown on a slave transport ship from Africa through the slave port of entry at Sullivan's Island at the mouth of Charleston Harbor. When emancipation came about in 1862, Jim Robinson and his family stayed there, working on the plantation, as free men and women but still enslaved by a system of economic oppression that has yet to be successfully addressed by the rest of society.

Fraser Robinson, Michelle Obama's grandfather, left the plantation in the 20th century and moved his family to Chicago. He returned to Georgetown in later years leaving their children and granddaughter in Chicago. It was from this background that Michelle Robinson went on to Princeton University in New Jersey, and then to Harvard Law School before she began practicing law in one of the nation's most prestigious law firms. It was there that she met her future husband who would become President of the United States.

Slavery, in all its forms and human deprivations, has made an indelible and positive impression on the rich culture of the Lowcountry. It is an impression that can never and should never be erased. Despite its horrific effects, however, it has undeniably contributed to making the Lowcountry the uniquely special place that it is—a crucial part of the *tout ensemble.*

SIX
SWIFT JUSTICE - SOUTHERN STYLE

*"In all criminal prosecutions,
the accused shall enjoy the right to a speedy and public trial..."*

~ Constitution of the United States, Amendment VI

Tyler Andrews

It was a nice spring morning in Charleston. There was plenty of sunshine, a gentle sea breeze, and moderate temperatures. The early morning noises were muted and pleasant.

African-American vendors walked through the streets in the downtown precincts almost every day. They sold fresh shrimp from door to door that they had just caught in nearby waters, and hawked vegetables they picked at dawn from their own gardens.

Charleston, an old South Carolina port city on the southeastern Atlantic coast, was founded in 1670 when the first English settlers and their slaves arrived from Barbados. There was much about the fabric of the city in the mid-20th century that had not changed since the founding. The city was full of ancient live oak trees draped with Spanish moss and, accentuating the tropical climate, there were abundant palm trees, called Palmettos, lining many of the streets. It was a sleepy port city, an easygoing place where ships from around the world occasionally called to drop off cargo and to sometimes pick up goods waiting on the docks to be distributed around the world. The crewmen of the merchant ships and sailors from visiting naval vessels were often the only intruders from the outside world seen wandering the streets of the insular community.

Throughout the town's long history, the inhabitants had been the blacks, now the descendants of the slaves that had been imported by the English, and the whites, whose ancestors immigrated from a variety of mostly western European countries.

Until the late 20th century, immigration from other places in the world was negligible. The white immigrants in the early years of the colony were mostly English, French, and Irish with fewer numbers of Germans and Jews added to the larger European and African mixture of humanity. The social system that existed in the mid-twentieth century resembled the South African institution of apartheid despite the emancipation of black slaves during the Civil War of the 1860s, and the 1954 decision of the United States Supreme Court which declared an end to racial segregation in public schools.

The system was one of complete racial separation, decreed by law and by the will of most of the white people. And it was there in Charleston harbor that the first hostile shots of the Civil War were taken against the United States.

In the 1960s, Charleston had not yet been discovered as a tourist destination as it would become in later years. It was a place of preserved buildings and southern gentility. Many, maybe most, of the people who lived there in the 1960s were descendants of the same families, black and white, who settled Carolina centuries before. The surroundings, the houses of the people who lived there, the streets, the gardens, the public buildings, seemed the same as they always had been.

The customs, traditions, and the closeness of the inhabitants of Charleston provided dependable groundings that made life predictable. There were few upsetting ripples in the social fabric, but occasionally something—or someone—would upset the balance.

There was another side to the equation, one small voice in a sea of inequality—a judge who came to the bench in the early 1940s determined to ignite the fire of racial equality. One of the few men appointed to judicial office whose later decisions surprised almost everyone because they deviated from all expectations. His name was Julius Waties Waring.

One of those surprises was his courageous attack on the inability of blacks in the South and beyond to vote in political party primary elections. The local white power structure had decreed that no black would be allowed to vote in a Democratic Party primary because it was a private party to which blacks were not invited.

This rule created a problem because in South Carolina only Democratic Party candidates appeared on general election ballots. There *was* no organized Republican Party.

Judge Waring decided and ruled that blacks should be allowed to vote in the primaries because it, in reality, was the general election and the right to vote for all citizens was guaranteed by the Constitution of the United States. For his trouble to do justice Judge Waring was effectively run out of town, but the law prevailed and his decision was never successfully challenged. In fact, a dissenting opinion of his in another case served as a basis for the unanimous opinion in the 1954 Supreme Court decision of *Brown v. Board of Education,* which declared an end to racial segregation in public schools and overruled the separate but equal doctrine for schools in America.

The call came about 10 o'clock on a Thursday morning in the spring of 1966. Langdon Gibbons answered the phone and recognized the familiar voice of Virginia Johnson, secretary to Judge Clarence Singletary. Judge Singletary was a state court judge assigned in this situation to preside over criminal cases in the local Court of General Sessions. Virginia immediately launched into the business of the moment, saying that a man named Tyler Andrews (not his real name for reasons of privacy) had been charged with the crime of rape.

"He has no lawyer," she said, "he cannot afford to hire one, he is entitled to have a lawyer, and the judge has just appointed you to represent him." Her voice, reaching the height of the message, said, "And the judge plans to call the case for trial at 10 a.m. next Monday morning."

Langdon sat there behind his desk stunned, still holding the telephone in his hands and trying to absorb what she had said. Twenty-six years old, had just finished law school in the spring of '64, and, after six months' active duty in the Army, had joined a prominent and respected Charleston law firm that practiced no criminal law.

He had never tried any case in court by himself, and certainly not a criminal one, so this assignment would be his first real one. Most of his knowledge of criminal law had been gained in a law school class on the subject taught by Dean Robert McCormick Figg, who coincidentally had represented the State of South Carolina on the losing side of the monumental case of *Brown v. Board of Education*. He had been the Solicitor (prosecuting attorney in the South Carolina criminal law system) in the Ninth Judicial Circuit before becoming the dean of the law school. Most of the sessions of Figg's class involved stories of his experiences in the criminal court. Langdon knew enough from what he had learned in his only law school criminal law course that the crime of rape carried the death penalty, but that and a familiarity with Figg's experiences hardly qualified him to defend a man's life in a criminal trial.

Langdon knew, too, that he had no choice—all lawyers in South Carolina in those days were eligible for appointment to represent indigents, without any compensation, in all criminal cases. There were no public defenders, and all defendants charged with capital crimes—as in this case—were entitled to representation. As it turned out, his name had been randomly selected from a list kept by the local circuit judge. There was no point complaining about his lack of competence or experience for the appointment—his only hope was reliance on the confidence and boldness of youth.

Terrifying thoughts raced through Langdon's mind. In a flash, he realized that a man's life had been placed in his hands, and there were three days to prepare. What to do first? Was this really happening? Langdon thought surely it was a bad dream from which he would soon awake.

"Oh," said Virginia, finally breaking the silence, "There are two more things I need to tell you about your assignment. The judge has appointed another lawyer with more experience to assist you. He has to appoint another lawyer because you have been practicing law for less than five years and the law requires in a case as serious as this one that someone with more experience be assigned to represent the defendant with you."

"Who," Langdon asked, "has he appointed?"

"Jack Drayton," she said. "And," she continued, "We've put your client in a holding cell down here at the courthouse this morning so you and Mr. Drayton can talk to him right away." He thanked her for calling and put the telephone in its cradle.

Although she hadn't said, Langdon knew instinctively that Tyler Andrews was black. It was the way the system worked. It would be unthinkable for a white man to be charged with rape on one day and be put on trial for his life three days later defended by lawyers whose names he didn't even know.

Despite the involvement of the older lawyer, Langdon was not comforted by the appointment of Jack Drayton, nor did it relieve his anxiety. Drayton was a crusty old fellow, a slick-looking thin-mustached character who smelled like the Wild Root Cream Oil he used to flatten his parted-down-the-middle curly gray hair.

Drayton was at least forty years Langdon's senior, a seasoned lawyer, but he too had little modern-day experience in the criminal courts. Drayton, Langdon suspected, would view this whole thing as a minor inconvenience, ignoring the clear sight of the electric chair their mutual client faced.

The word "crude" and "gauche" befitted Jack's personality and his language was reminiscent of the captains from sea stories from the days of the old sailing ships. Years later, when the news of Drayton's death made its rounds through the town, one of his colleagues allegedly remarked that he was so mean they'd have to screw his body into the ground to keep it there.

Still in shock, Langdon immediately called Drayton, who was expecting the call—he had already received the news from Ms. Johnson. When he said he was ready to walk with Langdon to the courthouse to pay a call on their new client, Langdon left his Broad Street office and met Drayton on the sidewalk. They exchanged a few words about their client's plight but talked mostly about theirs as they slowly made their way along the flagstone-paved sidewalk.

The Charleston County Courthouse was an old three-story square building at the corner of Broad and Meeting Streets in Charleston. The building sits on one quadrant of the intersection known as the "Four Corners of the Law." Saint Michael's Church, City Hall, and the United States Courthouse occupy the other three corners.

The courthouse building has a rich history. Built in 1753, it served as the South Carolina Statehouse until it was destroyed by fire in 1788. Rebuilt after the fire, it became the Courthouse for Charleston County, a function it continuously played until it was badly damaged by Hurricane Hugo in 1989. The building was put back in service as a courthouse following a complete renovation in 2001 which restored it to a design reflecting its long history.

At the time of the trial in 1966, the building was in a state of disrepair. Many of the plaster walls were cracked and the wooden floors worn or covered by cheap ugly carpet. Crowded into three floors were the entire criminal and civil courts of the county including chambers of the various judicial officials, the office of the Clerk of Court, the office of the Master in Equity, the Probate Court where estates were settled, the local office of the State Probation and Parole

Board, and the land record office, still called the Register of Mesne Conveyance, as it had been from colonial days.

Jack Drayton and Langdon took the rickety elevator to the third floor where the Solicitor's office and the holding cell were located. Reflecting the general peace and quiet that prevailed in the county at the time, prosecuting crimes was still a part-time job for the prosecuting attorneys. The Solicitor and three assistants, also part-time prosecutors, and one full-time secretary prosecuted every criminal case in Charleston and Berkeley counties.

Jack and Langdon announced their desire to see Tyler Andrews, and a police officer was called to escort them to a small room a few steps down a hallway. With people were milling about, there could be no privacy, and because there was no place to sit in the cell, so they all stood in a triangle just inside the cell door.

Andrews was a small man with dark brown skin and close-cropped curly black hair. Born a few miles south of Charleston, he had a heavy Gullah dialect. Jack and Langdon did their best to explain why they were there to see him. He seemed bewildered and apprehensive, naturally fearful that they were representatives of the same system that had put him in jail.

The conversation began slowly. All Langdon and Jack knew was that their client had been charged with the crime of rape. Jack asked Andrews why he thought he had been charged with rape, and after a few minutes of painfully pulling a few decipherable words from his mouth, Andrews said that he and his wife had had a fight and that she, in an act of retribution, had accused him of sexual activity with her daughter, now 15. Andrews said that he didn't do it, and said that his wife had made the whole thing up.

The three of them stood there in the small cell. Langdon shuffled back and forth from one foot to the other, nervously trying to decide what he should next say to the miserable-looking wretch standing in front of him, when out of nowhere, Jack began talking. Looking Andrews dead in the eyes, he said, "Boy, let me tell you one thing right now. If you don't confess your guilt to this crime, they're going to fry your ass. You've got to plead guilty to save your life. I mean it."

Tyler stood there without saying a word.

Langdon didn't know who was more afraid—him or their client. Newspaper headlines flashed in front of his eyes.

LAWYERS TELL CLIENT THAT HIS ASS WILL BE FRIED.

LAWYERS THREATEN CLIENT WITH DEATH TO AVOID A WEEKEND OF WORK

DEFENDANT SAYS CONFESSION AND PLEA WERE COERCED BY THREAT OF ELECTROCUTION

Battle lines had been drawn. Coercion and intimidation were things Langdon had heard about, but now he was right in the middle of it. They were now engaged in a two-front war, but the most alarming fact was that on one of the fronts, Langdon and Drayton were facing themselves as their own enemy. The other was, of course, the State of South Carolina.

Knowing that somehow he had to delay the trial, Langdon rushed out of Tyler's cell into the hallway to try to find Arthur Howe, the solicitor assigned to prosecute the case. He knew Howe was a good and decent man, and a good lawyer. The solicitor generally controlled the flow of the cases in the criminal court, and unless the judge had some special interest in a case, the solicitor's choice of what case to try almost always prevailed.

In Langdon's mind, Drayton's crazy statements to their client made a fair trial impossible, at least until the dust settled and some reasonable investigation of the facts of the case was conducted.

As he headed for the solicitor's office, it struck him that Drayton might have intentionally tried to create a situation where they would be disqualified from representing Tyler and not have to fool with the case at all, but either way, he realized that he and he alone had to somehow persuade Howe not to call Tyler's case for trial.

Langdon, whose sole object was now to get Howe to agree to postpone the trial, found the solicitor in the hallway near his office. Langdon knew that ethical principles would not permit him to reveal the reasons why he thought it had to be postponed—for reasons of attorney-client privilege, he could not tell him that Jack had threatened their client with the electric chair to coerce a guilty plea. Langdon had heard that defendants charged with serious crimes were often submitted to a thirty-day mental examination to determine their ability to stand trial, so he planned to throw that out to the solicitor.

So, in as plaintive a voice as he could muster, he told the solicitor that, for reasons he couldn't reveal, it would be impossible for Tyler's case to be tried on Monday or any other time soon.

Howe, who was quite experienced in his job, had heard almost everything there was to be heard from lawyers who wanted to delay justice and didn't seem bothered by the request at all. He seemed amused by Langdon's obvious state of panic, and patted the young lawyer on the back and told him not to worry about it—he would see that Tyler Andrews' case would not be called for trial on Monday.

The solicitor's reaction relieved Langdon's anxiety for the moment, but there was still the matter of how to go about defending his client. Thoughts raced through the young lawyer's head until he remembered a conversation with a longstanding judge from a county nearby. The judge had told Langdon what he'd come to believe, during his career before his appointment to the bench, was the most effective way to defend some of his criminal defendants—especially the guilty ones.

The judge explained that in those days in South Carolina, the only record of a charge was often the paper indictment handed down by a grand jury. A few investigative notes were generally folded and tucked inside the indictment and kept in the Solicitor's office files.

There was, he said, no other record of the charge, so if the indictment and its accompanying papers disappeared, there was a strong likelihood, almost a certainty, that the entire case would become lost in the system and forgotten.

He confessed that when he'd been retained to defend someone indicted by a grand jury, he had sometimes gone to the county solicitor's office and "stolen" the papers, and still had a few of those indictments securely locked in his safe at home.

But, he cautioned Langdon not to "steal" an indictment until he'd gotten the defendant released on bail. Otherwise, the prisoner might languish in jail until he died and the whole thing would end up as an unplanned life sentence.

Langdon considered the ploy as perhaps the only way to resolve Tyler's case and preserve justice. But he quickly rejected the idea and doubted that even Jack Drayton would dare to take that route.

Tyler's case was, as Howe had promised, placed on hold, and as time passed, Langdon decided the best defensive strategy was to avoid discussing it with the solicitor at all—unless Howe, God forbid, brought it up. He intentionally avoided going near the office over the next few months, but occasionally slipped into the solicitor's office when court was not in session, just to peek in the file cabinets to see if he could find what they'd done with the case. He never succeeded, but he knew something had to be done because Tyler was still in jail, and, as a good lawyer, he wanted to be prepared.

Summer now over, cool weather had descended, and with it the 1966 duck season. Mr. Billy Hanahan, the father of an old college classmate of Langdon's, invited him to shoot ducks on a Saturday morning at Dungannon, a Hanahan family country place in the southern part of Charleston County. He asked Langdon to meet him at 6 a.m. on the morning of the shoot at a store called "Marvin's Meats," near the little town of Hollywood. From there, they would go together to the duck pond.

When Langdon pulled into the parking lot of the store in his new Oldsmobile F-85 sedan, it was a little before six and it was clear but still dark and cold. The parking lot was about twenty-five yards from the paved road, so Langdon decided to turn his car around, and back up next to the store so he could stay warm in the car but still see "Mr. Billy" approaching.

As he backed the car in, his high beam headlights shone out toward the road and he saw a lone figure emerge from the darkness along the edge of the road. As the figure came into view, Langdon saw that the man was small, had dark brown skin and close-cropped curly black hair. And that there was something awfully familiar about the fellow. It was Tyler Andrews.

On the next Monday morning, as his first order of business, Langdon walked down to the courthouse — taking the same route that he and Jack had taken when they had paid their one and only visit to their client a few months earlier. When he reached the solicitor's office, he walked right up to the bank of filing cabinets, located the correct drawer, and began searching for the folder on his client. He was more anxious than ever to find out what had become of the case, not knowing if Tyler had been examined at the state mental hospital and was still a patient there, in jail pending a trial, or released on bail put up by some family member.

He rifled through the files, but in the end, he found absolutely nothing. There was no record at all that the case of the *State of South Carolina v. Tyler Andrews* had ever existed.

SEVEN
MARY DEAS

The slaves imported to America from other colonial settlements and from Africa constituted, by far, the largest group of immigrants to this country. All of them were involuntary immigrants, and they arrived in chains and shackles. They did not come here for religious freedom or for economic gain, as did many of the other colonizers. They were enslaved.

They and their descendants lived in these conditions for almost 200 years from the time of the first arrivals to the Carolina Colony before they were freed from legal bondage. But, the struggle for real freedom and equality that is guaranteed to all Americans by the Constitution of the United States continues in the 21st century. The stories of the struggles of Mary Deas for simple justice continued all her life for her and for millions of others like her. It is hard to understand why such struggling and endurance for basic human rights is necessary in what is advertised as a free society.

Mary was of the old school. In her case, it was a different old school than what one usually thinks about when the term is used—generally to explain a person's adherence to tradition. She came from slavery, just a generation removed.

This is not a story about the glorification of slavery because there is no glory in it. It is a story about the relationships of one woman who came out of slavery and the love she spread in the hearts of everyone she met. It is a story about a zenith of human virtues.

The deep nurture and loving care that enslaved women bestowed not only upon their children but also upon the children of their masters is one of those virtues. Besides caring for their own babies, the enslaved women were often surrogate mothers for the white babies in the towns and on the plantations of the Carolina Lowcountry. The slave mothers provided nourishing milk from their own breasts, a physical gesture that led to an affinity of spirit and compassion between the slave mothers and the children they fed. This practice became an indelible part of the ethos of the South that exists naturally even now as life extends from generation to generation.

Sometimes these slave-centered relationships were made even closer when the white master of the house or plantation impregnated a slave girl, enabling her to provide milk to her own baby as well as to the baby of the master's wife. In those situations, the slave mother gave the milk of life from her own body to the half-brothers and sisters, the family, all sired by the master of the place.

The practice of using what came to be called wet nurses in the southern United States and in the Carolina Lowcountry continued for decades that led to centuries. By the time slaves were emancipated in the 1860s, the practice had been established for almost 200 years. I'm convinced that the practice ingrained in the women a transcending quality of motherhood that might not have existed otherwise. It was a quality of intense nurture that translated into a deep love for the objects of the nurture, whether the children were biologically related or not; the babies they fed were inevitably strengthened physically and spiritually by these relationships. The quality of nurture and love acquired by these women and the babies they nourished was transmitted to their children and their children as generations rolled on, and it has smoothed the edges of the affection between the black and white natives who inhabit the Lowcountry. But as endearing as they may have been, they were nevertheless an offshoot of the inhumane and indefensible institution of human slavery, and its origins make it an unfortunate part of the legacy of the South. Mary Deas was one of the many women who bore the brunt of the cruelty with more dignity than most.

She was a strong woman, but her body was already showing the signs of aging when she came to help care for the children in the Gibbon's house in the late 1960s. The family house she worked in had two boys, one 2½ years old and another one on the way. Although she did some housework, a bad back limited the amount she was able to do. But she was strong in the ways that mattered most—the ways of the soul and spirit.

Mary was probably in her mid-60s when she joined the family. That would put her birth in the early years of the 20th century, perhaps around 1905 or so. All four of her grandparents and their ancestors for several generations had been slaves in the Lowcountry, yet she spoke with authority, especially to the children. There was never any doubt about where she stood on any issue.

Her frame was solid but not too tall, probably about 5'2", diminished somewhat by the natural aging process. Her hair was gray and close-cropped.

She and her husband, George, had no children of their own but they carefully nurtured an adopted daughter, Theresa, whose natural parentage was never revealed. About ten years old in 1960, she was a girl who just needed someone to take care of her and love her, and Mary assumed the mother's role—a role she voluntarily undertook and fulfilled until she took her last breath.

Mary exemplified the purity, the softness, and the inbred motherly instincts of all those hundreds of thousands who came before her. But, even 100 years after emancipation, society was still rough and unequal. Her natural disposition brought her spiritual happiness, but, at the same time, she was well aware that she lacked the respect to which every human being—indeed, every child of God—was entitled, and she had a yearning for justice and equality. But she found that the struggle from slavery to equality was a long road to travel.

Racial equality in practice is an elusive thing. The inequality of the races sank to the depths during the almost two hundred years when slavery was a legal institution in the United States and in many other countries around the world. When what was called "freedom" emerged during the Civil War, Mary Deas and millions of other human beings like her came out of it, but still at the bottom of the totem pole.

It has been a long, slow climb toward a level playing field, a goal that has yet to be reached. Human nature being what it is, the goal of racial equality has never and may never be reached, but the struggle will always continue.

When the American Civil War ended, the South entered an era called Reconstruction. At the beginning, the Southern white man was disenfranchised and the black man was enfranchised, but it was a short-lived arrangement. (Women, black or white, were not then even included in the system that meted out protection for civil rights.)

The enfranchisement of black men in the South led to the application of a basic law of physics—and of political science—that says the response to any action is always an opposing and usually equal reaction. But, in this case, the reaction was much stronger than the action to which it responded. The white man, able to garner greater economic and physical power, got his act together and set into place a system that became known as the Jim Crow era. The "free" black man was "put in his place" around 1870, and he has never been allowed to rise to equality since.

The dominant white man's plan via Jim Crow was to maintain as nearly as possible a complete separation of the races forever. There were lynchings all over the South well into the 20th century, often supervised by the Ku Klux Klan, an organization of unabashed white supremacists with free reign all over the countryside. They were ignored by the constituted legal authorities, often because those authorities were complicit in the oppression.

The plight of the black man in the South was dismal and uncivilized. This was true despite the fact that in places like the Lowcountry there were proportionately larger numbers of blacks in the population than most anywhere else in the United States. In the early days of the Klan, up until around the beginning of World War II, prominent, influential, and leading citizens all over the region were Klan members. A striking and stark example of that phenomenon was Hugo Black, who later outgrew his early racial views and became an eminent and great justice of the United States Supreme Court—ironically one of the nine justices who rendered the unanimous *Brown v. The Board of Education* decision. Justice Black turned out to be one of the most enlightened members of the Court. Unfortunately, although the decision declared the end of racial segregation in public schools in 1954, it has not yet been accomplished.

By the mid-twentieth century, the Klan became a fringe group comprised of mostly ignorant, lower class white men desperately trying to keep the black man in a subservient position. The apartheid model (the region's political leaders would never call it that in its day) was what the majority of the white post-emancipation society wanted. And, to a large extent, they achieved it. White people had all the economic power and controlled the education system—the two pieces of society that directly impact the quality of freedom and equality enjoyed by the people.

For starters, all black people were denied the right of access to any public accommodation used by white people. That meant that George and Mary Deas and their daughter, traveling through the South, could not sleep in a hotel or motel used by white people. That meant that Mary Deas and her family, even if accompanied by the family whose children she was nurturing, could not eat food in the same restaurant as her employer. It meant that Mary Deas could not use a water fountain in a public place that was provided for white people.

Mary Deas was required by her doctor to go to a waiting room set aside for the "colored." It was the same in train and bus stations.

Gasoline stations throughout the South often had three restrooms reserved for customer use—designated Men, Women, and Colored. When there was no colored restroom at a gasoline station, black people were denied the use of any restroom at all.

Mary Deas was required to sit in the rear of public buses if she wanted to ride a bus to work. She was required to sit in designated areas in the balconies of public movie houses if she wanted to watch a movie. Funeral homes in the 21st century Lowcountry were (and still are) almost completely segregated by race. So, too, were the churches, as Martin Luther King, Jr. pointed out—saying that a church on Sunday morning was the most segregated place in America.

All this was thought by many to be "the will of God." It was certainly the will of the people who made the laws that governed everyone—the will of the voters who, until relatively recent times, were almost all white men.

Much blood was shed in the late 1950s and '60s, mostly that of people seeking racial justice and those who tried to assist them in finding it. People died in Mississippi, cities were burned in California, children died inside churches bombed in Alabama, and black students were shot and killed by lawmen in the Carolina Lowcountry.

The truth of the matter is that in the first half of the 20th century, the life of Mary Deas wasn't very much different from apartheid. In the late 1940s and 50s federal judicial decisions began, little by little, to make a difference in the struggle for racial equality, but the problem of racial inequality by no means ended with the *Brown* decision. The court decision did, however, create a watershed of sorts that allowed people all over the country to focus on the problem of inequality as they never had before.

By the 1970s, some of the obvious and blatant racial oppression had disappeared, but not altogether. Most, but not all, white community leaders still found it inconvenient to be listed in the column of those supporting racial equality. It was unpopular and socially unacceptable. It was bad for business. It became a subject that was taboo for most people in the white community. These were the days in which organizations like the white Citizens Councils, masquerading as proponents of good government, were more devoted to the maintenance of the segregation of the races.

As a result, a more dangerous form of the disease of racism matured. It was one that was borne under cover—secrets that were whispered by some just as they gave lip service to equality—lip service aimed at exploiting the growing spending power of those previously relegated to the clear disadvantages of inequality.

Southern politicians were also quick to jump on the equality bandwagon in black communities when the franchise for voting was secured for blacks by law. Bounteous political lip service to racial equality, thanks to some early courageous court decisions in the South and national civil rights legislation leading to the Voting Rights Act in 1964, began to lead to meaningful reform in the national political system. The new electorate had spending power and voting power. It was a politician's dream world...votes available for the picking.

One by one the South's historically racist politicians were converted by the power of the ballot box. Some black leaders joked that the white politicians and others like them "got religion."

As history unfolded in the mid to late 20th century, racism was more subtle. It was harder to discern, but it was always there. As MLK said, the churches are an ironic example of lingering segregation. With few notable exceptions and token examples, the Southern churches of many denominations are not generally racially integrated even in the 21st century. There are, of course, ways to rationalize this situation — some of which have some legitimacy such as the argument that the difference in cultural values and interests lead people to different forms and styles of worship. However, it is nevertheless a fact that the practice of worship is divided along racial lines.

As late as the early 1970s, in an Episcopal Church in Charleston, South Carolina, several clean-shaven black men wearing coats and ties — all that would be expected in an Episcopal Church in the South of that era — presented themselves for admission just before the beginning of the main Sunday service at the front door of an historic "white" church on the Charleston peninsula.

The team of four or so ushers assigned to seat people for the service, a celebration of the Eucharist or the Lord's Supper, turned the black visitors away telling them that they were not welcome in the church.

The priest, who was about to begin the Eucharist, was informed of the incident just as the service began. When the ushers presented themselves at the altar rail to receive the sacrament of the body and blood of Christ — said by Christians all over the world to be the savior of all mankind — the priest turned the ushers away. They had, he said, publicly demonstrated that they were not in love and charity with their neighbors, a requirement imposed by the Church for receiving the sacrament. The action by the priest was indeed courageous — signifying that God's law prevails in the house of God no matter what men had to say.

In a democracy, voters ultimately make decisions that govern the lives of everyone. When the Lowcountry was settled in the late 17th century, the only eligible voters were white men who owned land. Until after the end of slavery, no black man was deemed by the society to be a human being in a legal sense and was generally classified as chattel or personal property.

Later, the franchise was extended to white men who were not real property owners. Women, incredibly in retrospect, could not vote until the United States Constitution was amended to allow them to vote in 1920, and they were not allowed to serve on a jury in South Carolina until sometime in the 1960s.

The right of blacks to vote was another issue all over the South in the 20th century. A citizen entitled to vote is a powerful citizen. A citizen without the right to vote has no control whatever over his own destiny or over the destiny of the society in which he lives. An effective way, then, of keeping the black man "in his place" was to devise and maintain a system that denied him the right to vote.

In the aftermath of the Civil War, the white men saw firsthand what it was like with empowered blacks electing themselves to public office in the void of disenfranchised whites. Undeterred by federal officials, those white men didn't take long to end the "abomination" and ride to the pinnacle of control of the ballot box once again.

Once black officials were ousted by the likes of the Ku Klux Klan, the white man had to invent various subterfuges to keep it that way. It was understood by practically everyone that the key to power was the ballot box, and to maintain power and control, the box had to be locked to keep blacks from participating in our system of government. If one has any sense of justice or compassion, it is hard to rationalize this treatment of blacks. What happened had no place in a civilized society. Their progenitors provided the lifeblood of the regional economy and many other aspects of the community for over 200 years.

But so it was. In the last few years of the 19th century, the State of South Carolina adopted laws that came to be known as "Jim Crow" laws. Much of the system of racial segregation (apartheid) was legalized by the State's Constitution of 1895. Among the laws adopted to control voting by black citizens was one that effectively barred voting by blacks in political party primaries.

Mary Deas and her family were effectively barred from participating in the public election process because of the color of their skin. The local rationale was that party primaries were "private clubs" controlled by the members (conveniently all white men), and they could decide who could vote in their party primary elections and who could not.

Today, such an arrangement may sound more fair and just than it actually was. Why? Because until after the mid-twentieth century, the Republican Party of Lincoln didn't even exist in South Carolina. In a severe Southern backlash against the party whose leader had freed the slaves, the Democratic Party was for all intents and purposes the only political party in the region. Deny access to the club, deny access to candidate choice. The Democratic Party primary was, for all intents and purposes, the general election because of a lack of opposition. So, unless one cast his vote in the Democratic primary elections, one's vote was worthless. The few Republicans in the state didn't want to participate in the Democratic Party's primary elections, and blacks and women couldn't, so it was business as usual in South Carolina.

Women were finally given the right to vote when the 19th amendment to the United States Constitution was ratified on August 26, 1920, but their right to vote in the South Carolina Democratic primaries and in the national elections was accorded only as long as they were white. So, even white women weren't allowed to sit on juries—the thought being that they needed to be at home cooking and taking care of the children and didn't have the quality of judgment men had.

It would be another 27 years after the ratification of the 19th Amendment before black men and women in South Carolina were allowed to vote in the Democratic primaries, and only then because of a lawsuit and a courageous judge—Charleston's United States District Judge Julius Waties Waring.

Why was the move courageous? Because Waring was a blueblood, a wearer of silk stockings who lived south of Broad Street at 61 Meeting Street. He was a neighbor of many other bluebloods in the historic district of the town. He was not only a descendant of Thomas Waties, one of the most prominent judges in the early days of the state following the Revolution, but also of John Rutledge, the second Chief Justice of the United States.

Waring was a part of the solid aristocracy who was raised with a silver spoon in his mouth and was not expected to rock the boat. Since he'd been sponsored by the state's two U.S. senators, Burnet Rhett Maybank and Olin D. Johnston, and appointed in 1942 to the lifetime judgeship by President Franklin Roosevelt, the last thing in the minds of people who knew Waties Waring was that he would order them to allow black citizens to vote in the Democratic Party primaries.

But that is what happened. And his courage gave Mary Deas, and the entire black population over the age of 21 years the right to vote, regardless of property ownership, regardless of gender, and regardless of skin color for the first time in the history of the Lowcountry.

In the beginning, when the trend of the judicial decisions set in place by Judge Waring began to take shape, many of the so-called South of Broad inhabitants believed the problem was not caused by his judicial and philosophical beliefs but by the undue influence imposed upon him by his wife. He had divorced his wife of 32 years at a time when divorce was not recognized in the state, and had married a "Yankee" woman. The extremes of opinion about Judge Waring are that he was either led down the primrose path by his new liberal wife to his ruin and to the ruin of everyone adversely affected by his court decisions or that he learned early in his judicial experience about the injustice and intolerance endemic in Southern society and decided on his own to do something about it. When it came to opinions, there was not much in between these two extremes, but, in the end, the truth prevailed. Judge Waring, quite by his own merit, saw the need to reform serious injustices that he faced in the courtroom.

The crowning blow came when Judge Waring rendered a decision in the case of *Elmore v. Rice* in 1947 that mandated that black people were entitled as a matter of legal right to vote in Democratic Party primaries. Local politics would never be the same again, and the entire political system was transformed by the decision. Its effect on local politics liberated the man, but sealed the coffin of Judge Waring in the minds of his local friends. But for the pro-segregation extremists, the worst was yet to come.

He issued a stinging dissent to the majority opinion of a three-judge court assembled to hear the 1951 case of *Briggs v. Elliott*, declaring that segregation of the races in public schools amounted to unconstitutional discrimination and was, *per se*, inequality. Although it was only a dissenting opinion, it would eventually have a very broad-reaching effect, providing the thrust of the unanimous *Brown* decision, which overruled, after 55 years, the 1899 case of *Plessy v. Ferguson*, which mandated the doctrine of separate but equal facilities as a way to deal with the racial issues in public schools. Although Waring was not credited for the result, it is credit he absolutely deserved.

Justice Waring's decisions were naturally welcomed and wildly popular in the black community, and were the subject of many celebratory meetings in the black churches all over the Lowcountry and around the country. But despite the celebrations, it would be a long time before people like Mary Deas would be relieved of more restrictive impositions on their legal rights.

As one might imagine, Judge Waring's behavior did not sit well with the South of Broad crowd. He was attacked in every imaginable way—social ostracism, attacks on his home, and maddening threats. All of it was serious business.

There were, however, a few humorous incidents. Jack Drayton, a lawyer, had a house on Sullivan's Island—an old-fashioned ocean front community of mostly summer residents of people who lived on the Charleston peninsula during the winter months. Judge Waring and his northern wife had a house next door to Jack's.

In the late 1940s, during one of the typical sub-tropical summer thunderstorms that usually hit the Lowcountry in the late afternoon,

Jack's beach house was struck by lightning and caught fire. During the night, after the fire was put out, someone put a prominent sign in Jack's yard near the street so it could be seen by passersby. The inscription read, "Oh, Lord, he lives next door."

When Jack told the story of the incident years later, he denied any complicity in the incident. Jack said that Judge Waring was upset about it, so much so that he summoned him to come to his Broad Street court chambers to discuss it. According to Jack, the judge wanted to know what he knew about who put the sign in his yard. Jack told the judge that he knew nothing about it.

The refusal of the so-called power structure to allow blacks to vote in the Democratic primary elections in South Carolina was only one of several methods used by the system to prevent them from exercising their right to vote. An early one was the imposition of the poll tax. Under that system, prospective voters were required to pay a $1 tax at least 30 days before an election. Whereas most white people could pay it, for former slaves it was more than they had to spare.

As it happens, South Carolina's poll tax was one of the more moderate of any in the Southern states, and it was repealed early in the 20th century. The tax was finally abolished for federal elections by a constitutional amendment in 1964.

Anyone who wished to register to vote in South Carolina, say in 1960—which was the year of the Kennedy-Nixon election for president of the country—had to go to the appropriate county Board of Voter Registration. There, a potential new voter was required to read and interpret that he or she understood an Article of the United States Constitution that was presented in written form.

In cases of individuals who, in the opinion of the clerk on duty, might have difficulty interpreting the section of the Constitution that was presented, there was a requirement that certain questions posed by the clerk to the applicant must be answered to the satisfaction of the clerk.

It should come as no surprise that many blacks faced this roadblock head on and often could not overcome it. Most young white college students, usually amazed by the process, were, of course, registered with no problem. Most of them had taken courses in Constitutional law or history in college and there had certainly been no descendants of former slaves in those classes.

So, how would Mary Deas approach the process of proving her right to attempt voter registration? For a while, it would not be a problem for her, because her first task would be to figure out how to overcome the fear and intimidation she knew she would feel. But she finally decided to "take the plunge" in 1971, when Lowcountry politics were thrown into turmoil and uncertainty after the sudden death of Lucius Mendel Rivers on January 21st.

Rivers had been the district's congressman since the middle of World War II and had served for many years as chairman of the House Armed Services Committee, one of the country's most powerful political positions. He held that committee chairmanship in the days when Southern congressmen wielded great power in the nation, heading up most of the committees in the House of Representatives.

At one point during his tenure as committee chairman, *Time Magazine* reported that Rivers's district, which covered most of the Carolina Lowcountry, was expected to sink under the weight of all the military installations that the Congressman had planted there.

Rivers's funeral was held at Grace Episcopal Church on Wentworth Street where the congressman was a communicant and in earlier times, a member of the choir. He attended the 8:00 a.m. Eucharist every Sunday when he was in town. His sudden and unexpected death during open heart surgery in Birmingham, Alabama began the overnight fast spinning of the political wheels in the district.

In short order, dates were set for the Democratic primary and after that a date for a general election to be held on April 27th to fill the vacant seat. The crowded field in the Democrat primary included the then Mayor of Charleston.

The Republican Party was steadily gaining strength, but it was not quite strong enough in 1971 to have a primary. Candidates who affiliated with Republicans were usually selected not by the voters at large but at a convention or by its Executive Committee.

Many in the vicinity of Charleston were motivated by the idea of helping the mayor of the city win the congressional seat and Mary Deas was inspired to vote for the first time in her life when she realized she might make a difference in the outcome of the election.

Some progress had been made in the quality of the process for the registration of blacks, and for everybody else for that matter, but it was certainly not the easy and effortless experience it should been. But it was better than in the days when constitutional interpretation by applicant was the requirement to be allowed to vote.

So, Mary boldly took the first shot at the registration office. Her first trip was unsuccessful because she did not have a driver's license to prove that she was who she said she was. Born before birth certificates were issued in the state of South Carolina, she was unable to provide one to prove identity. Some friends helped her obtain affidavits from people who had known her for decades, in hopes that the bureaucrats would accept them as proof of her identity.

After more wrangling with the bureaucrats, Langdon Gibbons called the chairman of the county legislative delegation who, in turn, called the chairman of the Voter Registration Board about Mary's plight. Mary was finally approved to be a voter and was issued a registration certificate.

How many people who had the legal right to vote could possibly have gone through what Mary did to accomplish such a feat? How many continue to be deprived of their rights of citizenship today?

After the polls closed at 7 p.m. on the day of the primary, Langdon, interested in the outcome of the election for the congressional seat up for grabs for the first time since World War II. He decided to walk down to the county courthouse where the votes were counted to see how things were going.

Everything was moving along smoothly at election headquarters, and the mayor was doing well in the Charleston precincts that had reported, but it was clear he would have to wait to find out what was happening in the congressional race—its outcome could not be predicted until returns were received from other counties in the district.

After a while, John Graham Altman, a local lawyer and poll worker from the precinct where Mary was registered to vote came in and saw Langdon across the room. Knowing about his friendship with Mary, Altman wandered over and said to him, "Mary Deas presented herself to vote at our precinct today, but her name was not on the registration list."

Langdon lashed out. It was unthinkable, after all the time and effort he and she had expended to get her registered, to have once again been denied, he said.

Altman raised his hand. "Wait a minute, Langdon. I didn't say she didn't *vote*. I just said her name was not on the registration list."

Langdon's eyes narrowed. "How in the world could she vote if her name was not on the registration list?"

"Well," said Altman, leaning in, "she said she worked for you and that was enough for us, so we let her vote in the name of Henry Scrughan, deceased."

Mary Deas, just one in a long line of nurturing, struggling women of the Lowcountry, finally made it and cast her ballot against all odds. A stalwart representative of people like her in a long line that began in 1670 in the Lowcountry, she was a rich contributor to the heritage of all of us who will ever live there.

She is gone now, and it is high time for those following in her line to be given an uncontested seat at the table.

EIGHT
FREDERICK CORNELL JENKINS

Much of the world we live in is invisible to most of us, but it is there and we live in it, seen or unseen. Frederick Cornell Jenkins lives not in that invisible world, but between that world and the one that most people inhabit. He dwells in a place that can be visible, but it is unlike any place that most of humanity has ever seen. Outside our understanding and experience, his world is a world between worlds.

It was a beautiful spring Saturday in 1998, at 7:30 in the morning. Langdon was beginning his usual walk when he met Mr. Jenkins for the first time.

While Langdon was wearing his exercise clothes, Mr. Jenkins was dressed in a nicely tailored suit, a tie around his neck, and a fashionable fedora covering most of his closely cropped dark hair. Stopping directly in front of Langdon, Jenkins quietly asked if he could give him a couple of dollars to buy a cup of coffee. Langdon had no money with him so he simply said, running his right hand up and down the plane of his clothing, "I have no money with me." Nodding, Mr. Jenkins calmly continued on his way down King Street.

A few hours later, as Langdon was walking through the crowd at the Charleston Farmer's Market—about six blocks north of their first meeting—he spotted Jenkins milling about amidst the crowd.

A tall, imposing statue of John C. Calhoun presides over this portion of Charleston's historic landscape. It is a commanding presence. The market stalls are along either side of paths within Marion Square. Two rows of stalls are set within a triangle-shaped area framed by the intersection of King and Calhoun Streets. A seasonal, weekend institution occurs here. Fresh fruits and all sorts of other food, crafts and the like are sold from small tents placed along the paths by farmers and other local merchants.

When Langdon spotted him across the crowd he could see he was dressed the same as he had been earlier in the day. Langdon was in his Saturday casual clothing and now had some money in his pocket. Instinctively, Langdon walked toward Jenkins. "I'm sorry I didn't have any money with me when you approached me this morning," he said, "so here's five dollars to get yourself some coffee and a sandwich."

Smiling, Jenkins took it and simply said, "Thank you."

Since that first meeting he and Langdon have learned a lot about each other, but Langdon has clearly learned much more about Jenkins than the other way around. A friendship slowly took root over many years, and from this relationship, Langdon learned the remarkable story of his life.

Why am I telling it? The answer is for the reader to decide. No matter the answer, it will be clear that this is the story of one life that proves the durability of the human spirit and its ability to prevail despite overwhelming odds.

Frederick Cornell Jenkins, a gentle man, is a son of Charleston to the core of his being. He is a part of it and it is a part of him. Although Cornell, the name he is known by most of his friends and family, is missing some of his teeth now, his voice is warm, strong, and clear. His skin is dark and coffee-colored, and his hair is closely cropped and graying. He looks a good bit older than his 67 years.

When he speaks, his eyes sometimes appear to be almost closed. At other times, they are wide open and sparkling. His mobility has been affected by a limitation of the use of his legs. This condition causes him to walk with a shuffling gait. Sometimes he uses a cane to help him along.

Sighting Cornell in the street offers the beholder a unique vision and a special treat. The observer sees a man who wears his pride as comfortably as he does his signature coat, tie, and proper gentleman's hat. He appears impeccably attired from early morning until mid-afternoon when he customarily heads back to his abode in North Charleston.

The truth is that Cornell knows a lot about men's fashion and pays particular attention to what those around him are wearing. During one of their many early morning conversations, Langdon and Mr. Jenkins, the name by which Langdon always addresses him, were sitting across from one another at a Starbucks table on King Street. Mr. Jenkins, looking down, noticed that a flap on Langdon's jacket was slightly askew and said to him in a quiet, gentle voice, "Langdon, straighten the flap on your jacket pocket." On another such occasion, he showed up for one of their regular meetings at Starbucks without his usual coat and tie—dressed in jeans, a denim shirt, donning a broad brimmed hat and wearing a red bandanna knotted around his neck. Langdon said to him, "Mr. Jenkins, looks like you're been on the range this morning."

Cornell firmly responded, "I'm on the range every day."

Some of what is revealed here about his life comes from an autobiography he began writing sometime in 2010, but most is based upon what he told Langdon in many conversations spanning several months in 2011 and 2012.

Most of their meetings have been at a Starbucks at 239 King Street in Charleston, six or seven city blocks south of his birthplace and two blocks north of the site of their first encounter.

About a year after they learned each other's names, Cornell told Langdon, "I am going to begin writing my autobiography this day." As he uttered the words "this day," he pointed emphatically into the air with his right index finger.

Langdon said, "Mr. Jenkins, if you are going to do that, you will need to get a pencil and some paper." To which Cornell responded, again emphatically, "I am going to do that this morning." And he did.

He bought some pencils and a few spiral notebooks and began writing. Langdon did not inquire about his progress during the ensuing months, nor did he press him for results, but accepted occasional updates from him about it. In February of 2012, he had almost filled the first book, and he told Langdon that as soon as he did, he planned to give it to him.

Two days later he handed it to him, and on the first page was written: "Langdon, All Rights Reserved With All my Love Frederick Cornell Jenkins."

Here we are.

Early Life

Mr. Jenkins was born into an African-American family on Judith Street in Charleston on November 15, 1947. The house he lived in for the first few years of his life is not there anymore. He says it was numbered either 2 or 9 Judith Street; he's not sure which. It was, as he describes it, "a small wooden cabin that was torn down to make way for a mansion for some white people to live in."

Judith Street is in a part of Charleston just north of Calhoun Street running east to west across Meeting Street in a part of town called Wraggborough. It's not far, two or three blocks, from the Charleston Farmers Market.

The street got its name from one of the daughters of Joseph Wragg, the owner of an urban estate in the neighborhood for which his son John laid out the streets in 1801. The streets in the neighborhood are named for all of Joseph Wragg's children: John, Judith, Mary, Ann, Charlotte, Elizabeth, and Henrietta, and they are all still there in the 21st century with the same names. It was Cornell's childhood neighborhood.

A chart of his genealogy over just three generations would look like an elaborate maze—who came from whom and who belongs to who is confusing. But, here's just a taste of it.

His mother was Ophelia Jenkins, and his father Frederick Wright. They're gone now. Frederick Cornell, Cassandra, and Linwood Leroy used the name Jenkins. Kalvin Angelo, Wanda, Victoria, and George were the children of his mother and George Bennett. Of his mother Ophelia's seven children, Linwood Leroy and Wanda have died, leaving four who are alive in 2016.

Cornell has lived in Charleston most of his life. Some of his years have been spent away in New York. Some have been spent in a residential home for mental patients in the Piedmont region of South Carolina, some in a mental hospital in Chicago, and some in a mental hospital in New York.

But he's been in or near Charleston since just before Langdon first encountered him. A brother, Kalvin Angelo Bennett, called Andy, is in Atlanta where he is working as a tax return preparer and studying for a master's degree in law; George Dwayne Bennett was released from jail on February 16, 2012, having served a three-year sentence for grand larceny; and the sister, Victoria Bennett, teaches in the public schools in New York, while living on 111th Street in Harlem.

He is the only child his mother had with Frederick Wright, to whom she was probably not married. He, the first child of Ophelia, was taken as a young child to Ebenezer AME Church on Nassau Street in Charleston where he was baptized.

The father of the two other children is unknown, but they used the surname Jenkins. The Jenkins family lived in Georgetown, South Carolina until after Ophelia's father's death when Essie, her mother, moved to Charleston with her children. Samuel and Essie's four children were Cornell's mother, Ophelia, Samuel, Elizabeth, and Dot Jenkins. Essie married Wesley Mitchell soon after she arrived in Charleston. Their two children were Alvin and Jerome Mitchell who were Ophelia's half-brothers.

Cornell's mother, Ophelia Jenkins Bennett, died in New York in 1998. His father, Frederick Wright, was a Charleston native but spent a career of many years in the U.S. Army where he was a cook. He achieved the enlisted rank of master sergeant.

Cornell says he saw his father only three times before his death in Los Angeles in 2000. The first two of the meetings with him, when Cornell was six and 14 years old, were at his mother's apartment in New York. The third brief meeting was in Charleston at his aunt Rachel Wright's house where his father was visiting while on leave from the Army. At the time of the last meeting, Cornell was 23 or 24 years old. Of that visit, Cornell said, "The only thing he ever gave me in his life was $20 when I saw him at Aunt Rachel's house."

Life for Cornell was rough from the beginning. To define it as dysfunctional would be an understatement.

It began without any adult supervision. He says he roamed alone around the Judith Street neighborhood from the time he learned to walk. He said that he has no recollection of meeting or even seeing his mother until he was six years old. The first meeting was at the home of his aunt Elizabeth Jenkins Frazier, near the space now occupied by the Gaillard Auditorium.

In another conversation with Langdon, Cornell said, "In those days of my life my grandmother and others in my family walked in the spirit, not physically." When asked to explain what he meant by that description he said, "Well, you knew people were there around you, but you could not see them. You could feel their presence as they brushed by you."

He has no idea about who fed or clothed him for the first six years of his life. The only name he remembers from those days is someone named Ronnie, who he sometimes saw in a house on St. Philip Street near the College of Charleston. But he has no idea who this person was or how he was connected to the family, if indeed he was at all. Everything about Ronnie remains a mystery.

The "wooden cabin," as he refers to the house on Judith Street, was his home or his base of operation until 1953. Beginning in 1953, the family, such as it was, lived in his aunt's house at 69 Calhoun Street at the corner of Alexander. It was in that house that he has the first memory of his mother. He said, "My life really began in that house, and I began to learn about myself for the first time."

That same year Cornell was united with his larger family at the Calhoun Street house, Ophelia married George Bennett and moved with him to New York. She left Cornell in Charleston with his grandmother, Essie Jenkins Mitchell. Bennett, according to Cornell, was a musician living in Charleston, a trumpeter playing in bands around town.

The New York Years

Ophelia decided to move to New York in the summer of 1960. She and Cornell left on a Greyhound bus for what he thought was going to be a short summer vacation. As it turned out, he did not return to Charleston for three years.

During this phase of his life, Cornell lived with his mother and his siblings on 128th Street between Lennox and Fifth Avenues in Harlem. By then, Ophelia and George Bennett had two children of their own. Bennett abandoned her and the children in 1960, and told Cornell as he left the house, "Cornell, you are now the head of the family."

Cornell was enrolled in Seward Park High School, on the Lower

East Side of Manhattan, and attended there until he returned to Charleston in 1963. Ophelia was at home drawing welfare and earning some money taking care of children for working mothers. Cornell soon got a part-time after-school job washing dishes at a nearby hospital.

He really didn't like New York. And, at age 16 he decided more or less on his own to come back to Charleston. Back home, he moved in with his grandmother, Essie Mitchell, at 12 Line Street near the new road called the Cross Town—U.S. Highway 17. It runs from the Ashley River bridge linking James Island to the peninsula and leads to the Cooper River bridge (now the Arthur Ravenel, Jr. Bridge) and Mount Pleasant on the other side.

The family's move from Calhoun Street to Line Street came about because of the creeping gentrification. Essie Jenkins Mitchell and her family were displaced, along with many other black families, from the site of the new Gaillard Auditorium, which takes up an entire city block. There have been almost no black families living south of Calhoun Street since then.

Cornell enrolled in the 10th grade at C.A. Brown High School where he was admittedly not a good student. A year later, he decided to go back to New York and rejoin his mother and siblings. There he once again enrolled at Seward Park High School and working part-time as a dishwasher at a Jewish hospital on 106th Street. He then worked for about six months as a stock clerk at Lord and Taylor on 5th Avenue.

It was during this stretch in New York that he became interested in the Nation of Islam. It was an encounter that would guide and direct much of the rest of his life.

Cornell became friends with Patrick X, a young man about his age who lived in the neighborhood. They began to spend a lot of time together and their friendship led to conversations about the Nation of Islam. Patrick, as it turned out, was already an enthusiastic adherent of the movement.

Cornell explains that Patrick X evangelized him quite persistently, and his pushy salesmanship led to Cornell's own involvement in the movement. When Cornell joined the Nation of Islam, it was an organization headed by Elijah Muhammad whose origins were in Sandersville, Georgia where he had been a sharecropper.

Born Elijah Robert Poole, he and his wife decided to leave Georgia in 1923 to settle near Detroit. Their reason for leaving the South was, as Elijah Poole has written, to avoid the oppressive Jim Crow laws that had sprung up in the South. He wrote, "I seen enough of the white man's brutality to last me 26,000 years."

Once in Michigan, Elijah came under the influence of Wallace D. Fard, later Wallace Muhammad, who led the new organization based on Islamic teachings and the added goal of black empowerment in America. Fard had spent three years in Mecca where he said he learned all he knew from Allah. "He," according to Cornell, "passed on everything he had learned in Mecca to Elijah Muhammad."

When Fard mysteriously disappeared in 1934, Elijah Muhammad took control of what would become known as the Nation of Islam. Elijah's younger brother Kalot Muhammad became the leader of a division called the Fruit of Islam, described as the Nation of Islam's self-defense arm. Under Elijah's leadership, the Nation of Islam developed temples, as central places of activity and worship, in all the largest northern cities. By 1950, there were 50 Temples in 20 states.

Patrick X soon prevailed upon Cornell to attend events with him at the Temple in New York City. On his first visit to the Temple, the speaker for the evening program was Louis Farrakhan. That experience hooked him, and he was swallowed by an infatuation with the Nation of Islam that has not yet waned, although his days as an active participant are over.

He and Patrick developed a routine of attending functions there on Wednesday, Friday, and Sunday of each week, where they were taught the precepts of freedom, justice, and equality by a Captain Youseff. "Youseff," Cornell says, is an Islamic name for "Joe."

The Saturday teaching sessions he and Patrick X attended were called Fruit of Islam and were led by Farrakhan, who succeeded Malcolm X as head of all the temples in the New York region and later became head of the global organization, with over 130 temples and mosques in America and the world.

In a conversation at the Starbucks, Cornell explained to Langdon that he was given the name Cornell X. When asked what the "X" in one's name signified, he said that it was meant to erase the surname of the person who had adopted Islam.

When Langdon asked about why this was done he said, "The last name of every black person in America is nothing but a slave name, a name coming out of the time of slavery in America. The X gets rid of it."

He further explained that he was later given a more formal name, authorized by The Honorable Elijah Muhammad. The name bestowed on him then was Rasool Shair Muhammad. At this point, Cornell said, "I am now a nomad Sunni because I do not follow the strict Islamic rules for living."

"What rule, for example, don't you follow?" asked Langdon.

"I smoke cigarettes," he answered.

"The Honorable Elijah Muhammad," said Cornell, "was the supreme leader of the Nation of Islam, and everything that any member did had to be approved by him."

Cornell explained his relationship with Louis Farrakhan at the New York Temple this way. "Farrakhan," he said, "taught us every Saturday morning with the *Quran* in one hand and the Holy Bible in the other. I was in his presence for three years. Early in my visits to the Temple, I bought a copy of the *Quran* for $10 at a bookstore on 7th Avenue."

Cornell's routine participation in the structure of the Nation of Islam was that after their classroom and training sessions, he and Patrick X were sent out from the Temple to sell copies of the Nation's weekly newspaper, *Final Call*, formerly known as *Muhammad Speaks*. He and Patrick X sold most of their papers in the Times Square area around 42nd Street and 7th Avenue, but he said, "Minister Farrakhan told us that The Honorable Elijah Muhammad said our newspaper was not for white people, and we were told not to sell it to them."

Cornell became enraged by what he considered to be an unreasonable and unfair limitation on their newspaper selling activity and in 1966, at age 19, he got on a bus and headed alone to Chicago to personally address his grievance with The Honorable Elijah Muhammad.

Once in Chicago, Cornell found the house where Elijah Muhammad lived and sought to see him there. Raymond Sharif, the Supreme Captain in the Nation of Islam, refused to allow him to speak with the leader. He was intercepted outside the house and turned away.

Cornell explained, "I did not have a lapel button identifying me as a member of the NOI and, without the identification, they would not let me in. I failed in my effort to see our leader The Honorable Elijah Muhammad."

For reasons that no one knows or can explain, Cornell's life dramatically changed forever at that moment. He was suddenly and inexplicably overtaken by paranoid schizophrenia, a disease defined as uncontrolled fear marked by a disconnection between thought, feelings, and actions. He told Langdon that he thought then and there that someone was trying to kill him. He has been told by physicians and believes that this disease formed in his early life and was dormant in his body. Why? His reaction to this suddenly emerging condition was to take off his shirt and shoes and to dive headlong into the Chicago River...in complete panic and in an effort to escape from what he did not know or understand. With this action, a long nightmare began for him.

Cornell finally swam out of the river on his own. He says he ran as fast as he could for miles, trying to escape from whatever it was that was chasing him. After several miles of running as fast as his feet would carry him, he was "grabbed" by the police, like a deer caught in headlights, and was taken by an emergency medical vehicle to the Illinois State Psychiatric Institute where he was a patient for 90 days.

This was to be the first of 28 hospitalizations for Cornell, most of them involuntary. At the onset of this long and tragic road, Ophelia was notified of these events and came to Chicago to try to help. She soon discovered that she also was helpless to do anything about what was happening and left Cornell there and returned to New York.

When he was discharged after the 90-day stay, in a remission of some sort, he was able to return to New York by himself and there joined his mother and siblings, who then lived in Brooklyn.

Upon his return to his family, Cornell got a job at Sterling Regal, an engraving company on 7th Avenue in Manhattan—not far from the United Nations Plaza He worked there for about six months until the storm clouds of his illness once again began to gather.

The development and availability of medicine for mental illnesses was in its infancy in 1966. When Cornell was released from the Chicago hospital he was simply put out on the street to wait for the next episode of his illness to overtake him. He was not prescribed any medicine at all to ward off the certainty of the future attacks of his illness.

After a few months at home, his mother began to realize that he just didn't look good and she took him to see a physician. This consultation led to his second hospitalization. This time he was admitted to Kings Park Hospital in Kings Park, New York for three months, and was again put out on the street without medication.

In those days, there were few medicines to successfully control it. Cornell said his doctors have told him that the disease he has usually manifests itself between the ages of 19 and 25 and that it is caused by a chemical imbalance in the brain. His was a classic case.

The Homecoming

Soon after his release from Kings Park, Cornell decided to come back to Charleston, arriving in 1968 and taking up residence with his grandmother, Essie Jenkins Mitchell, at 85 Alexander Street. He got a job pretty quickly at the S&S Cafeteria on St. Philip Street, just five or six blocks from his grandmother's house. He lasted for two weeks.

He soon got another job as a janitor at The Citadel, The Military College of South Carolina. He held that job for about three months.

Then, not long after his arrival in Charleston, Cornell got into serious trouble with the law for the first time. He stole some blank bank checks from Viola D. Norman, who lived in the neighborhood near his grandmother's Alexander Street residence. He filled in the blanks on some of the checks and tried to cash them at a grocery store on Columbus Street.

His brazen and crude attempt to get ahead in the world became a federal case, and charges were brought against him. His lawyer, Russell Brown, was able to work out a resolution of the charges for him, and Cornell was sentenced to a term of five years probation — narrowly escaping jail time.

In the wake of the attempts to hold down a regular job and the settlement of the federal charges, he finally found a job in Charleston that he knew something about. For three years beginning in 1970 or 1971, Cornell sold editions of *The Chronicle*, a start-up weekly newspaper published for the African-American community.

His mental illness, without the aid of any medication to control it, simply made it impossible for him to conform to the demands of a regular job. In 1973, Cornell adopted a new form of activity—a career of street preaching, espousing the tenets of the Nation of Islam at the corner of Reid and America Streets in Charleston. It was during this time in his life that Cornell intensified his devotion to the brand of Islam he learned in New York. He engaged in evangelism on the streets of Charleston on behalf of the cause espoused by the

Honorable Elijah Muhammad and Minister Louis Farrakhan for the Nation of Islam. It was during this period of his evangelizing in Charleston that Minister Louis Farrakhan authorized Cornell to bestow Islamic names on followers he brought to the faith. For this purpose, Farrakhan sent him what Cornell calls a Book of Names.

This book contained a long list of available names, separated by gender, for him to choose from to fit the situation. The names were bestowed on new adherents to the faith of the Nation of Islam much like names are bestowed at the time of baptism in many Christian churches.

When a name was given to a follower, it was removed from the book so that it would not be used again. Cornell said he handled the cases of pregnant women a little differently. Explaining the process to Langdon he said, "You know in those days there was no way to look into a woman's stomach to see whether it was a boy or a girl. So, I gave the pregnant women two names from the book, one for a male and one for a female. After the baby was born, the mother could name the child using the appropriate one for its sex and discard the one not used."

He believes that he gave out about 40 names using the book on the streets of Charleston. Now he wonders how the usage of those same names has multiplied in the many years since they were given to the parents and grandparents of current inhabitants of the city.

When not street preaching, Cornell engaged in an entrepreneurial project he developed to sell men's clothing on the streets of Charleston. The start-up capital for his venture came in the form of a cash gift of $200 from William Ackerman, a Charleston lawyer. Ackerman ran for mayor of the city in 1971 and was narrowly defeated by Palmer Gaillard, the incumbent. Despite his narrow loss, Bill Ackerman gained the support of a large majority of the burgeoning black community that almost carried him to victory. He was known by many to be a generous man, and in that spirit gave Cornell the $200 he needed to establish himself in the retail trade on the streets of the city.

Cornell immediately applied for and received a peddler's license from the city fathers for the established fee of $30 and began to acquire an inventory of men's clothing to sell on the streets. He explained how he was able to acquire goods to sell from a number of wholesale houses operated by Jews on East Bay and Meeting streets just a little south of Market Street. One of them was Hyman's Wholesale on Meeting Street, located in a building that now houses Hyman's Seafood restaurant, a popular local restaurant mostly catering to the tourist trade.

Cornell carried men's clothing, mostly hosiery and underwear and shirts, all in a box with a strap attached to it that he could rest on his shoulder. As a complementary service to the clothing sales, Cornell revived a service that he offered in Charleston in earlier years—to block hats for gentlemen. He took the hats given to him to his grandmother's at 85 Alexander Street and blocked them overnight for a fee of $10. The hat blocking business dwindled in the wake of changing men's fashion trends, and that part of his business became a small part of what he did as the wearing of felt hats by men had drifted out of fashion.

Cornell began preaching Islam in earnest on the corner of Reid and America streets. He stood on the corner near a house his grandfather had built years before. It was now the home of his aunt Toots Jenkins Singleton and a cousin, Dot Jenkins White.

When Langdon asked him to explain why he selected that particular site for preaching, he said, "It was a short walk north on Alexander Street to the corner of America and Reid from where I lived in the family house at 85 Alexander. And, the people in the America Street neighborhood were interested in Islam, and that's what I wanted to preach about. I preached there every day for three years except when they had me locked up."

The trouble began there during the preaching episodes from 1973 to 1976, and it has never ended. He said the drugs, mostly heroin, were everywhere in that part of town, and that he was able to get some of the brothers off of it by winning them over to Islam because it forbade any use of drugs.

Cornell says he knows of at least two people he preached to on America Street whom he saved from the horrible depths of heroin addiction. He converted them to Islam, gave them Islamic names, saving them from the ravages of the drug.

One of them was Ismail Shabazz, a name bestowed on him by Elijah Muhammad through Cornell, replacing Larry Reid, which had been his name prior to his conversion to the Nation of Islam. Ismail overcame the heroin addiction and lives today on Amherst Street where he grew up. "Ismail is free of drugs, doesn't drink or smoke now, and he don't eat no pork," says Cornell. The other convert, Abdul Kareem Shabazz, formerly Jerome Reid, also overcame his addiction but met a violent death in 1976 when a neighborhood shopkeeper shot him to death.

Cornell said Abdul's murderer was a man named Steve who owned a shop at the corner of Reid and America Streets. It was a pool hall, snack bar, and a place for the young people to hang out, but it was very rough. Steve, Cornell says, slept in a little room in the back of the shop. "Abdul's murder was not an isolated event," he said. "Steve shot him with a shotgun, and he was not the only one he shot. He shot many people there for no reason."

"How," Langdon asked, "could he get away with all that shooting?"

"I don't know, but he was never arrested for killing Abdul, and he shot a lot more people right there before he shot Abdul. I went to the hospital that night with him, but he was dead on arrival. After Abdul's murder, Steve fled to somewhere in the lower part of the county and nothing was ever done about it. After he left some people burned his shop to the ground. It's still a vacant lot right now. There's a big sign on the lot with pictures of children on it.

"Dot Singleton, my cousin, was irritated all the time by the preaching. She couldn't stand it and had me arrested and locked up for doing it. They put me in shackles and hauled me off. The first time was in 1975 when they arrested me and sent me to Bull Street [the South Carolina Mental Hospital that was located on Bull Street in Columbia, the state's capital city and called Bull Street by most everybody in the state old enough to remember it].

"I was there for seven months that first time, and it was the first of what turned out to be twenty-eight involuntary hospital admissions up in Columbia over the next few years."

When asked why his cousin had called the police, he replied, "I don't know why she did it. She just did. She didn't like what I was doing. I always preached Islam. The people in the neighborhood and passersbys all called me Brother Muhammad. She's stingy as hell too."

These frequent hospitalizations continued — all of them in the State Hospital on Bull Street in Columbia. There was no genuinely effective treatment for the schizophrenia Cornell suffered from. They arrested him for the street preaching, hauled him off to Bull Street with a Probate Court order, locked him up for a minimum of 30 days, sent him home, and from there the pattern repeated itself. This endless routine began to change in the 1980s when two important trends set in.

Treatment for the schizophrenia improved when newly developed medication, properly administered, made hospitalization unnecessary. Armed with that advancement in the science of treating mentally ill people, the state began to arrange outpatient care for the mentally ill. Frederick Cornell Jenkins was caught in this wave of change, and it changed his life for the good. But, it was not good for most mentally ill people because the hospitals were closed, creating a serious problem caring for those who needed institutional treatment. It is a problem that still exists in America.

In 1984, Cornell was assigned a caseworker employed by the South Carolina Department of Social Services, supported by federal funding, to see that he got the medical care he needed outside the hospital. Residential care houses were organized to provide supervised housing for those who could not live at home or had no home, as was the case with Cornell.

Cornell was assigned to such a residential care house in Greenville, South Carolina in 1984 where he lived in a relatively normal but supervised environment. His last hospitalization, of 30 days, occurred while he was living in Greenville. He was taken to a hospital in Anderson when a spike in the symptoms of his schizophrenia could not be controlled by medication at the residential home. That was the last time for him in any hospital from then until now.

Soon after his last hospitalization in 1986, Cornell's caseworker transferred him to another residential care house in Laurens, a town not far from Greenville. Cornell was in residence there for twelve years.

"It was strict," he says. "There were 12 rooms, two to a room, and we all had to do chores every day. A woman named Rolanda Glenn was in charge, and she was a tough taskmaster. She worked for the owner, a Ms. Doyle who we occasionally saw. We were given a place to sleep, three meals a day, and $30 a month for spending money. They administered our medicine every day so we didn't have to worry about it."

It was while he lived in Laurens that he attended a Baptist church and was there baptized for the second time. While living in the residential home, he became friends with someone named Brenda who introduced him to the church where he was baptized.

Life took a big turn for Cornell in early 1998 when he was sent by his state Department of Social Services caretakers to live in the city of his birth—the city he loves, Charleston. Feeling bad about his absence of almost 15 years, he has not left Charleston County for one minute since his 1998 arrival and says he never will.

He was moved around a bit from one residence house to another for the first few years after his homecoming. First, he lived at a place in the Ferndale neighborhood of the city of North Charleston. It is a city that is in a geographic area just north of and bordering the city of Charleston, an extension of the Charleston peninsula to the north. Ferndale is a little east of Rivers Avenue and just south of the Mark Clark Expressway, another name for Interstate 526.

After a year at Bell's Residence on Delta Street in Ferndale, he was moved for a year to a place a little more northward with the colorful name of April Showers. Then in 2002, there was another move to a similar residence on Redwood Street in the same general area, but further to the south, and very close, about two blocks, from Evergreen on Norwood Street. He has lived there since 2006.

Evergreen is organized to accommodate 40 people segregated by gender. The men sleep on one side of the house and the women on the other and use separate bathrooms for each gender. The three meals that are served each day are eaten in a common dining room.

Cornell's stipend from the state, after receiving his meals and place to sleep with two roommates, is now $40 a month. Asked about his relationship with his roommates, Cornell says they get along all right but don't talk much. He describes the arrangement at Evergreen as "independent living."

One spring day as Langdon was walking up King Street returning from lunch, he found Cornell sitting on a bench outside Birlant's Antiques waiting for the bus to take him home for the evening. Langdon joined him on the bench. He complained about the dressing habits of tourists, especially the men, as they watched a horse-drawn wagon-load of them passing by. He said he was thankful that they — he and Langdon — held to the traditional style.

When Langdon asked what that would be, Cornell quickly replied, "A coat and tie at all times outside the house." As they were talking, a saleswoman from Birlant's came out of the store, on cue it seemed, and gave him a couple of magazines. One of them was a popular local magazine called *Charleston Living*.

As in most of the real cities in the world, life on the streets is usually interesting and robust. It is not unusual when Cornell and Langdon talk on the street in front of Birlant's or a block further north in front of Old Town Restaurant for them to be joined by other characters.

One day while they were chatting, a fellow by the name of George Gordon showed up. Gordon lives in the neighborhood and is often seen walking to or from the restaurant 82 Queen Street, where he has coffee and reads interesting books.

George always wears a nice straw or felt hat, depending on the time of year, and always carries in one hand the book he's reading. His sin is that he invariably wears short pants, a habit that upsets Cornell.

A few days later, in the early morning, Cornell and Langdon were talking while sitting on the bench in front of Old Town Restaurant when Father Gregory Wilson showed up and joined the conversation. Now the pastor at a large Roman Catholic parish in Aiken, South Carolina, until recently, Father Wilson was the pastor of the Cathedral of St. John the Baptist just around the corner on Broad Street. An old friend of Langdon's from his days at the Cathedral, Father Wilson is a fine young priest.

Langdon politely introduced him to Cornell, saying, "Mr. Jenkins, this is Father Wilson, and he is a very good man who you need to get to know."

Cornell replied, "Langdon, anyone who is a friend of yours is a friend of mine." At that, Father Wilson smiled. The priest and Langdon went for coffee and Langdon told the priest a little about Cornell's life history. He seemed especially affected by Cornell's relationship with the Nation of Islam and the background of his mental illness. So it goes.

Another leg of Cornell's business venture involved selling rare coins. He explains that there was a coin shop in the old Heart of Charleston Motel at 200 Meeting Street that has now been gone for many years. There he was able to acquire a few coins from the shop for what he thought were good prices to resell to people in the streets. All this commercial activity complemented his now burgeoning panhandling operation—one he had learned and practiced on the streets since boyhood.

Cornell's business interests reflect, even now, his personal interests. Upholding his own standards for dress, it is rare for him to venture out of his living place without a coat, tie, and hat. He usually wears a suit of matching trousers and jacket. He now has an extensive collection of magazines. One of his favorites is the *Ben Silver* catalog. New editions of it are regularly produced by the high style and successful clothing company headquartered at 149 King Street. It is not unusual for Cornell to take one of his catalogs out of his briefcase and spread it on the table as he and Langdon drink their early morning coffee during their many conversations at Starbucks.

Early in 2012, Cornell told Langdon he needed a copy of the *Quran* and had been looking around for one but they were too expensive at the Barnes & Noble College of Charleston Bookstore. He asked Langdon to try to get him one and he did, ordering it from Amazon. Cornell told Langdon that the edition he'd selected for him was the best in the English language. He said it was something he "desperately needed." As soon as he got the *Quran* he told Langdon he also needed a copy of the *Bible,* a King James Version, red letter edition. Langdon got him one of those too from Amazon and gave it to him on January 31. While Cornell was living at Laurens, he read the Bible ten times, cover to cover. His recall of biblical passages important to human behavior is nothing short of remarkable. He often recites many of them during some of his conversations with Langdon. His ability to provide specific citations for most of them is astounding. Langdon was surprised when he checked the accuracy of what Cornell quoted — almost verbatim from the King James version of the *Bible*.

"In this world, you need to know the right people, but don't be greedy. Moderation is necessary. Both the *Quran* and the *Bible* say 'Help the poor.' Read Proverbs Chapters 6 and 7. It says, 'Give to those who don't have.'" He talked about the generosity of King Solomon and how he gave money away "by the bus load, looking out for other people, and also recognizing the need to take care of oneself." He told Langdon all should read The Acts of the Apostles 20:35, which he then quoted: "I have given you all things, and you should help the weak…and, remembering the words of the Lord Jesus, it is more blessed to give than to receive." He then suggested that it would be good for Langdon to read the 7th chapter of the Gospel according to Matthew, and referred to where it says, "Ask and it will be given to you; knock and the door will be opened for you. For everyone who asks receives, and everyone who searches finds, and for everyone who knocks, the door will be opened."

All this, of course, begs the question of how Cornell squares Islam and Christianity. The truth seems to be that he sees the good and truth in both, a powerful lesson indeed. There is no doubt, one gathers, from Langdon's many conversations with him that the brand of Islam represented by the Nation of Islam for Cornell has a lot to do with the issues of racial injustice springing from slavery in the United States. It involves righting the wrongs that have been perpetrated by whites against those of African descent in America.

In his autobiography, Cornell has written a lot about these issues. Some of it is quite vitriolic. On the other hand, he said one morning in the spring of 2012 that he knew Jesus was his "Lord and Savior." It is a dual allegiance for him to two great spiritual traditions, but to the same God. For him, they co-exist within one another. Both are important and, for him, both are true. "I recognize," he says, "that no one possesses all the truth."

Each day, Cornell rises about 3 a.m. and reads and writes until dawn. Usually skipping breakfast, Cornell then gets on CARTA, a regional transportation bus system, and heads to downtown Charleston. In Charleston proper, Cornell generally frequents, as described earlier, an area not far from where he was born and grew up. He fans out in various directions from the City Market to visit friends and supporters, many of whom, like Langdon, help him supplement his meager income, often on a regular basis. Honoring a tradition that he says he's been doing since the age of seven, he regularly engages in what he and the city police authorities call "panhandling," a practice that he and the city police have had differing views as to its legality.

Despite this, Cornell always seems to approach a stranger, usually a tourist, and politely and gently asks for a financial contribution, just as he did when Langdon first met him. On these occasions, which are almost daily, he is always properly attired in a coat and tie, and a nicely blocked felt hat or a straw one in the summer months. He says that, with the exception of his years of exile, this has been his regular routine and practice in Charleston for 57 years.

The way has not always been easy. Not long ago, Langdon encountered Cornell as he was, once again, walking north on King Street near its intersection with Market. He had not seen him in several weeks.

When asked where he'd been, his response was, "In jail."

"For what?"

"Panhandling again, 30 days this time."

Langdon shook his head. "Mr. Jenkins, you need to let us know when that happens so we can assemble a defense team."

"Yes," he said, "but it's hard to make a call from up there.

He looked good after the stint in the tank and was in good spirits. He didn't seem to mind it too much.

The police were beginning a concerted effort to make him stop soliciting people for money on the downtown streets. It appeared the city was also trying to keep him from going into certain areas downtown where they deemed he would not be welcome.

This sort of police enforcement in Charleston is not altogether new. In fact, Cornell has been arrested 13 times or so since his return to the city for Soliciting for a Charity Without a Permit and, more recently, for trespassing. Following these historic arrests, he has served about seven 30-day sentences for total jail time of nearly 210 days.

After some considerable pressure from Susan Dunn, an excellent lawyer representing Cornell, the city repealed its prohibition against panhandling, except at locations next to highways and intersections, and Mr. Jenkins now legally and peacefully plies his trade every day.

Through it all, however, despite long and continuous stints living in jails, hospitals, and social service houses, Mr. Jenkins has maintained his high lifestyle standards. Dressed in a coat and tie and wearing a hat every day he strolls the streets of Charleston giving others authoritative advice on all sorts of matter whenever needed.

In fact, just this past spring, Langdon, dressed in his somewhat shabby exercise clothes, sat down next to him on a King Street bench in the early morning hours. After glancing around, Mr. Jenkins discreetly leaned over and whispered into his longtime friend's ear, "Langdon, you need to remember that style and grace are important."

And so it is.

Frederick Cornell Jenkins is a descendant of slaves who by the sweat of their brows molded the Lowcountry of South Carolina from the raw materials provided by nature and made it what it is. He is a gentleman who has experienced life in ways few humans have. He has embraced and appreciated two of the great religions of the world and uses them as his guide, recognizing eternal truth in both. He has overcome the ravages of mental illness with steadfast determination. He has developed and enjoyed more lasting friendships than most of his fellow countrymen. And his life, despite many and frequent hurdles and hardships, endures in a good spirit from day to day. He lives at the core of the essence of the Lowcountry and it is his world. That is why this book is dedicated to him.

PART III

NINE
THE FRENCH

French people came to settle in the Carolina Lowcountry in three distinct waves of immigration in the 17th and 18th centuries. As in the case of the English settlers, few of them came directly from their homeland. Connected only by their national origin, the arrival in Carolina of three groups of French people spanned more than a hundred years beginning in 1680.

The first Gallic arrivals were French Protestants. The Huguenots, as they were called, were a small minority in a France which was largely Roman Catholic, and generally intolerant of other religious persuasions. The Huguenots' beliefs were based upon the precepts of the theologian John Calvin, whose followers were a part of the Protestant Reformation that began in Europe in the early 16th century. Calvin was born in France in 1509, emigrated to Geneva in 1532, and became a major figure in the Protestant Reformation.

Beginning in about 1562, religious wars were waged in France by Roman Catholics who, of course, were opposed to the Protestant Reformation and its accompanying religious toleration. Much of the fighting that continued to the end of the century took place in western France around La Rochelle, Ile de Re, Rouen, Bordeaux, and Tours where many of the Huguenots lived. There are even today burned-out church buildings standing on the Ile de Re as evidence of the conflict. There was intermittent emigration throughout the century by Huguenots seeking to escape the effects of religious persecution, and it intensified as the wars with the Catholics ensued during the last third of the century. Most of the 16th-century emigration was to other European countries that included England, Switzerland, and the German states until the colonization of North America began.

The pressure to emigrate subsided in 1598, when the destructive religious wars ended and Henry IV of France, himself a Protestant who converted to Roman Catholicism, decreed the Edict of Nantes, granting religious freedom to the Huguenots. But as time passed the political pressure on the Huguenots in France to conform to Roman Catholicism intensified again, and emigration increased as the 17th century progressed. The majority of those leaving France for religious reasons continued to settle in other European countries. This time, however, some emigrated to North America. Among the first to arrive were those who accompanied the Dutch when they settled New York in 1624.

Religious and legal rights of Huguenots who remained in France came to a screeching halt in 1685 when Louis XIV promulgated the Edict of Fontainebleau, revoking the Edict of Nantes.

There were approximately 750,000 Protestants in France in

1685, less than 5% of the nation's population who not only lost their religious rights but were also stripped their legal protective rights. They, in effect, became non-persons in the eyes of the Sun King and his government. Three options became available to Huguenots when the Edict of Fontainebleau was decreed by the king. A Huguenot could convert to Roman Catholicism (about 550,000 did) or one could openly resist (about 2,500 did and most of them were imprisoned or went underground) or one could flee the country (about 200,000 did).

The issue of religious toleration in France was more or less settled for the next 100 years when, in 1787, Louis XVI decreed the Edict of Toleration on the eve of the French Revolution. The Revolution also promoted religious diversity throughout the country but on entirely different terms than were decreed by the royal government. The revolutionaries installed a non-Christian-based religion based upon the mythological history of the ancient Roman gods.

The first Huguenot immigration began just ten years after the founding of the English colony at Charles Towne—the first Frenchmen to attempt a settlement in Carolina since the failed Carolina colonization project in 1630.

This group of Huguenots left London on December 17, 1679, aboard the ship Richmond, made a call at Barbados—as the English had done a decade earlier. They arrived to join the English settlers at Oyster Point on the Ashley River on April 30, 1680. These Huguenots, about 45 of them, all came from England, where they had fled in the years leading up to the Revocation of the Edict of Nantes. Recruited by the Lords Proprietors, they became a part of the English scheme for colonial development, which was to provide staples for the national economy centered in London and raw materials for the English mills.

After achieving clear early success, the Huguenots soon came to the Lowcountry in greater numbers. By 1700, there were between 500 and 600 Huguenot settlers in the colony.

A smaller number of Huguenots came from Switzerland in 1731, and more came in the 1760s to settle New Bordeaux on the Savannah River, which separated South Carolina and Georgia. Although the numbers of Huguenot settlers were a small proportion of the 200,000 who had fled France, they comprised the largest number in the North American colonies. More than 1,000 arrived in the Lowcountry before the beginning of the American Revolution.

Most of them were merchants, artisans, and farmers. They became founders of the important rice and indigo cultures of the region, developed a strong business dealing in naval stores, and, as might be expected, engaged in the emerging slave trade. The Lowcountry Huguenots assumed important positions in the social, political, and religious life of the community. Even in the 21st century in the Lowcountry, the influence of the Huguenot settlers is carried on by their many descendants.

Of the 14 significant Huguenot settlements in North America, six of them were in the Carolina Colony: Charles Towne, the new home for 200 Huguenot colonists; the Santee River basin where 110 settlers made their new life; the Orange quarter where Jacob Guerard and René Petit were early community leaders with 100 fellow settlers; and Goose Creek where 30 Huguenots settled. These were the most important centers of Huguenot immigration in the Lowcountry.

The other two, Purrysburg and New Bordeaux, were on the

Savannah River in the western part of the colony. Huguenots never represented more than about 15% of the colonial population, and, over time, were completely assimilated into the community. They participated in the colonial government, became members of the Anglican Church when they lost their ecclesiastical identity by the Church Act of 1706, and supported the removal of the Lords Proprietors from governmental authority in 1719. Many of the Lowcountry English merchants became loyalists, but almost all of the Huguenots supported the separatists in the Revolutionary War.

As stated, they were completely integrated into every aspect of life in the colony. However, Lowcountry settlers organized and maintained the Huguenot Society, a cultural and genealogical organization that keeps the heritage alive. Many of the Huguenot names are prominent in the Lowcountry in modern times: Gaillard, Legare, Porcher, Huger, Manigault, Rembert, Cuttino (Cotheneau), Ravenel, Guerard, de Saussure, Marion, and Petit are but a few of them.

While some historians contend the tenets of religious freedom were the foundation on which our country's settlement was based, it is the Huguenots who represent one of the few immigrant groups who left their native country to immigrate to other countries to avoid religious persecution, and then engaged to become part of the Lowcountry's colonial settlements.

The Acadians, largely Roman Catholics, were the second distinct group of French people to immigrate to the Carolina Lowcountry. Their immigration, however, was neither voluntary nor lasting.

A little more than a thousand Acadians were expelled from Nova Scotia and more or less "dumped" in the Lowcountry in 1755 by the

British. Thousands of them were moved from Nova Scotia to various places in the southern colonies. The reason they were transplanted was that the British feared that they would be a security threat in Nova Scotia where the French and Indian War was proceeding in full force and the British were fighting the French for domination of the continent.

The Acadians did not assimilate into the community of the Carolina settlements. They were beset by disease and continuing migration so that there is no identifiable vestige of them remaining in the Lowcountry of the 21st century. They received no local support, and the few that did eventually settle in the region became indentured servants.

European political divisions played out quite favorably for the Americans during the American War of Independence. The conflict between England and France was likely the major catalyst of French support of the American colonists, which proved vital to the success of the revolution. Most historians of the period agree that without the French intervention, the outcome of the struggle would probably have been quite different.

The first sign of the French involvement began on the ground in America when LaFayette arrived at Prospect Hill, a plantation of the Huguenot Benjamin Huger on the banks of Winyah Bay at Georgetown, South Carolina.

Marie Joseph Paul Yves Roch Gilbert du Motier, Marquis de LaFayette was born on September 6, 1757, and married to Adrienne de Noailles on April 11, 1774. She was 14 years five months old on the day of the wedding; he was sixteen years and six months, two years and a month older than his bride.

Soon consumed with a passion to serve France and the American revolutionaries across the Atlantic, he sailed, commanding his ship Victoire, from the west coast of France across the Bay of Biscay toward America on April 20, 1777. They dropped anchor in Winyah Bay in the early afternoon of June 13th. LaFayette's first act on American soil was to take an oath that he would vanquish the British or perish with the American cause.

The Frenchmen were received at Prospect Hill by its owner, Major Benjamin Huger, who took LaFayette and his officers by land to Charleston. The crew of the Victoire sailed the 60 miles down the Carolina coast to meet their captain at the Charleston port. In February 1778, LaFayette and Baron de Kalb, another officer who had been aboard the Victoire, were soon enrolled as major generals in the Continental Army of the United States. Lafayette is likely the only 19-year-old directly commissioned as a major general in the army.

Le Marquis de LaFayette became a close personal friend of General Washington and a trusted comrade in arms. He was at Washington's side at the surrender of Lord Cornwallis and the British at Yorktown, the final decisive victory of the Americans in the Revolution. At the birth of one of his sons on October 79, 1787, LaFayette named the child George Washington de LaFayette.

Although LaFayette is the symbolic figurehead of France's support of the American cause, there were others who made heroic contributions on behalf of Louis XVI and the people of France.

Jean-Baptiste, Comte de Rochambeau, a general of the northern Army in America, also served under Washington's command in the Continental Army. He marched his army of about 5,000 troops to Yorktown, a movement that contributed to the British defeat.

François Joseph Paul, le marquis de Grasse, a fleet admiral, sailed his ships with another 5,000 troops aboard from Saint Dominique to meet the British at Yorktown. De Grasse debarked the soldiers on shore to join those of Washington and LaFayette while the ships of the fleet blocked the harbor and prevented a premature departure by the British forces. By these acts and the involvement by French forces, the American victory at the end of a long war was secured.

This opened the floodgates. Thousands of French immigrants came to the southern United States near the end of the 18th century when the bellicose effects of the French Revolution reached the French colonial island of Saint Domingue in 1793.

The ratio of slave to owner there was about ten to one on the island. Massive slave uprisings led to the ascendance of Toussaint l'Overture, a former slave who became the revolutionary leader of the new island government, which ended white domination and gave rise to what is now the nation of Haiti. This slave uprising led to the displacement of up to 20,000 white colonists, some black slaves, and mulattoes who fled to the United States to escape death and destruction at the hands of the new regime.

The massive emigration began on June 23, 1793, when 400 vessels were assembled in the harbor at Le Cap on the northern shore of the island. Most of the ships set sail for the United States, but others went to France and other islands in the Caribbean. Charleston, the center of the Carolina Lowcountry, was one of four southern United States ports for which the ships departing Saint Domingue set sail with their cargoes of fleeing Frenchmen and their slaves. The other port cities were New Orleans, Norfolk, and Baltimore. The whites who left the island were almost all Royalists, Roman Catholics, and slave owners.

The French

In 1793, Charleston was a city of about 8,000 whites, 8,000 slaves, and 600 free blacks. On the heels of the American Revolution, the city was a center of revolutionary sympathy, but the Royalist sentiments and religious persuasion of the 500 new arrivals from Saint Domingue did not prevent their warm reception by the citizens of Charleston. In fact, the duc de La Rochefoucauld-Liancourl, a notable French Royalist who spent much of the period of the French Revolution in the United States, reported that Charleston was the most hospitable city in the country.

The immigration of Frenchmen from the Caribbean islands continued at a slower pace in the years following 1793 until 1808 when about 250 French immigrants arrived in Charleston from Cuba. The latest arrivals had been living in the Spanish colony since fleeing Saint Domingue, and were run out of Cuba by the Spanish colonial government after France's attack on Spain during the Napoleonic Wars. In all, 7,323 Frenchmen fled Cuba for various places in the United States during the Franco-Spanish Napoleonic hostilities.

Most of the French immigrants who came to Charleston between 1790 and 1808 arrived destitute, usually with only the clothes on their backs to begin their life in the promising new country. Citizens of Charleston accepted them with open arms, caring for their most basic needs. In 1793, the townspeople collected $12,500 to help support the immigrants, and the next year the federal government appropriated $15,000 to aid the French immigrants from Saint Domingue of which $1750 was sent directly to Charleston. Local officials reported that the town had about 300 to 400 French immigrants that needed public support, and urged that 30 pounds sterling was annually needed for the support of each adult immigrant, and 15 pounds for each child.

The South Carolina General Assembly appropriated 3,000 pounds sterling for food for starving people in Saint Domingue.

New arrivals from Saint Domingue gave the Carolina Lowcountry a breath of much needed fresh air. This most recent immigration of Frenchmen came more than a hundred years after the first English settlers arrived from Barbados. Early Huguenot arrivals had been assimilated, and the American Revolution had come and gone. The Lowcountry, as well as the rest of the country, had become thoroughly Americanized. The English colonial government had been replaced by one based on a written constitution created by Americans.

The English church, although still prevalent in the urban coastal cities, had given way much of its earlier dominance in the Backcountry to the Methodism of John Wesley, the Baptist theology of Richard Furman, and to Scotch-Irish Presbyterianism. There was no longer a state church, and such a development was important for the French immigrants.

The world these Frenchmen entered into in the Lowcountry was one that had little contact with the European world and one that had become set in its ways. Civic institutions in the former colony had become a little dull and dusty.

The wave of immigrants from Saint Domingue included aristocrats who owned plantations and slaves, army and naval officers, colonial officials, professional men, and tradesmen. There were merchants, planters, artisans, artists, and many slaves. There were men trained in the social graces and manners, something that was absent in the general population except in the upper levels of society. The skills represented by these new immigrants not only changed life in

Charleston and the Lowcountry, but also in the other cities along the eastern seaboard where they settled.

It was the same in New Orleans, Norfolk, and Baltimore. Frances Sergeant Childs in her book, *French Refugee Life in the United States, 1790-1800: An American Chapter of the French Revolution* said, "The refugees introduced into America many French traits; a logical mind, intelligence, religious and artistic sensibility."

These new immigrants brought with them to the Lowcountry expertise in dancing, fencing, music, opera, language, cooking, and fashionable dress. Before long, Creole French was heard spoken throughout the city of Charleston, where there were streets like King, Archdale, and Union entirely filled with French shops, and French dress. In this area, the French language was often preferred to English.

One of the most colorful characters of the era, Simon Felix Gallagher, a professor of French at the College of Charleston, came to serve as one of the early priests for The Church of St. Mary of the Annunciation. The growth of the Roman Catholic Church sparked by the French and Irish immigration soon led to the formation of the Diocese of Charleston and led to its receiving its first bishop, John England, an Irishman who arrived in 1820 from Cork in Ireland.

French immigration from the Caribbean brought many interesting people to the Lowcountry. Charleston, suddenly and with little advance notice, became a city full of talented and experienced people across a wide spectrum of community life. There were among them merchants, mariners, carpenters, physicians, bakers, cigar makers, bookkeepers, jewelers, silversmiths, musicians, tailors, and coach makers.

Philip Stanislaus Noisette, a botanist and horticulturist, left an indelible legacy in the Lowcountry. He developed a variety of the rose called Noisette. He lived for a time at the Sword Gate House on Legare Street in Charleston and was director of the South Carolina Medical Society's botanical gardens. Louis and Heloise Budol were notable silversmiths, and Peter E. B. Raynal was an accomplished goldsmith. Dancing and music instruction were available from eight immigrant masters including Theodore B. Fayolle. A theater was established by the French immigrants to offer drama and opera.

Many new schools for the children of Charleston were opened. Among the most popular were those of Julia Datty and her niece, Rose Talvande, who operated her school first at 102 Tradd Street, and then on Broad Street, before moving it to The Sword Gate House on Legare Street. It was in the school at the Sword Gate House that the famous Civil War diarist Mary Boykin Chesnut studied, and where Bishop John England dined weekly.

Among the immigrants were the five children of Admiral François Joseph Paul de Grasse, the French naval officer who sailed from Santo Domingo in 1781 to help Americans defeat the British and Cornwallis. One of the children, Alexandre François, became an architect in the city. Proficient in landscaping and fortification design, he was also a fencing master. One of his daughters married a fellow immigrant, François de Peau, and the other married John Grochan. Both lived the rest of their lives in Charleston. Two other of his daughters died at young ages of yellow fever—their bodies are interred in the Saint Mary's churchyard.

Another expatriated Frenchman, Charles Balthazar Julien Fevret de Saint-Memin, came to Charleston when he was prevented by the 1793 island uprising from visiting his mother, a Saint Dominigue creole. A renowned painter of miniatures in the 18th and early 19th century, he would leave behind over 760 examples of his work in towns and cities and towns up and down the east coast of the United States. The method he used for his miniatures was called *physionotrace*, a technique by which he produced a pantograph on red paper and then painted in the exact features of the subject's hair and clothing. Saint-Memin variously lived in Charleston, Richmond, Annapolis, Washington, and New York, and painted miniatures of many of the prominent citizens in all the places he visited and lived.

Monsieur Le Fevre arrived in Charleston, but left his slave, Antoine, to manage his plantation in Saint Dominigue. Antoine exported produce from the plantation to Le Fevre in Charleston.

Theodore Gaujan de Maurney, a graduate of the Sorbonne, and a Paris lawyer before taking up residence in Saint Dominigue, fled to Charleston and is buried in the Saint Mary's churchyard.

The Ramousin family came to Charleston with their slaves and opened a music store at 30 Beaufain Street. French army general John B. De Caraduc brought 30 slaves and a quantity of diamonds with him from Saint Dominigue. He sold the diamonds to members of the South Carolina Alston family, and bought a plantation in Saint Thomas Parish with the money from the sale. The Lachicotte family with their children acquired numerous plantations—Cedar Grove, Waverly, Willbrook, and The Tavaern—on the Atlantic coast north of Charleston. The family is still, in the 21st century, prominent in the life of the community on the Waccamaw Neck, the region north of Georgetown along the coast.

French institutions were founded in the Lowcountry. Social clubs included La Société Française. There were several coffee houses that included Vauxhall Gardens at 44 Broad Street, the Lafayette, the Carolina Coffee House, and the Coffeehouse of Louis Chupein. French language newspapers were formed in the Lowcountry, including *La Patriote Français* that was founded in 1795 and published by Claudius Beleurgey; and *L'Oracle, Français-Americain*, founded in 1807.

Militia units stationed in Charleston, reflecting the revolutionary spirit of its recent history as a reaction to earlier British colonial domination, wore uniforms modeled on those of the National Guard of Paris at the time of the French Revolution. Architecture of the Lowcountry, in the cities and in the countryside exhibited a style that reflected both its Caribbean Spanish and French origins. The architecture of the famous Charleston single house design has clear similarities to house designs of the French West Indies.

French immigrants arriving in the Lowcountry in the late 18th and early 19th centuries were greeted by their Huguenot countrymen and English Barbadian predecessors from the earlier immigration to the colony. Their cultural contributions to the life of the region and their influence on the life of the community were indelible.

Important hallmarks of the French Lowcountry culture were courtesy and charm. These attributes combined with the solid English governmental institutions and the longstanding agricultural economy gave rise to the development of a society that became the envy of the rest of the nation.

It has endured throughout Charleston's history.

TEN
A FRENCH PRIEST IN CHARLESTON

The Roman Catholic Church had a slow beginning in the Lowcountry because the English colonial government prohibited the immigration of any Catholic to the Colony of Carolina. The exclusion of Catholics was not altogether a result of theological disagreements or disputes about religious beliefs. It was mostly a reflection of European political disputes.

Catholics began to filter into South Carolina only after the British were defeated in the American Revolution and the 1789 ratification of the United States Constitution, which protected the establishment and free exercise of religion, including Roman Catholicism.

Early Catholic immigrants to South Carolina came mostly from European countries, and they were predominantly Irish, French, and Dutch. There were enough Catholics in Charleston in 1788 to form a parish, and Saint Mary of the Annunciation was founded on Hasell Street. Since its founding, it has been an active parish of what has been since 1820 the Diocese of Charleston. Saint Mary's became the first parish between Baltimore, the leading Catholic city in America at the time, and New Orleans, an old French settlement. After its establishment, other parishes were soon organized in other cities along the Atlantic Seaboard, including in Richmond, Virginia, Wilmington, North Carolina, and Savannah, Georgia.

Although a parish had been established, until many years after the end of the American Revolution, there was no diocese or bishop south of Baltimore. In Charleston, a committee of elected trustees provided government for the parish. Trustees were chosen to represent the interests and desires of the predominantly French, Irish, and Dutch members of the parish.

In the absence of a bishop to guide the fledgling congregation, the affairs of the parish were conducted by the lay trustees in ways that did not conform to established ecclesiastical rules but were more often influenced by secular and ethnic considerations. Because of this perceived lax administration by the parish trustees, Saint Mary's was from time to time placed under an interdict by the episcopal authorities in Baltimore. This meant that the congregation was forbidden to operate as a parish of the Roman Catholic Church until reforms in its operational behavior were implemented to conform to church imposed rules and regulations. These circumstances often led to turmoil and disorder in the affairs of St. Mary's, and the authorities in Baltimore soon recognized that something needed to be done to stabilize its clerical management.

Appointed pastor of Saint Mary's by Archbishop John Carroll of Baltimore, The Reverend Simon Felix Gallagher arrived in Charleston in 1793. He followed several short-term priests who had administered the parish since its founding in 1788. Archbishop Carroll was far away in Baltimore, and Saint Mary's suffered from the lack of the close episcopal authority it needed to be a successful and traditional parish of the Church.

The bishop thought Father Gallagher possessed the qualities the parish needed to stabilize its conformity to standard church practices so he sent him to the Lowcountry. Gallagher had been a priest of the Diocese of Dublin, and Carroll thought his degree from the University of Paris, the Sorbonne, would appeal to the French communicants.

In November 1812, a newly ordained priest, Joseph-Pierre Picot de Limoëlan de Clorivière, arrived in Charleston to assist at the local parish. Father Gallagher had already established himself as a part of the growing brotherhood of eccentric characters in the town so the new arrival fit nicely into the mix. Father de Clorivière, age 44, added considerable zest to the mixture of eccentric and interesting personalities inhabiting the Holy City.

It didn't take long for storm clouds to gather as routine complaints began to make their way to the archbishop in Baltimore from some of the communicants of the parish. A persistent complaint concerned Gallagher's lack of sobriety while conducting Masses at St. Mary's. Despite the growing number of complaints about his personal behavior, however, Gallagher made many contributions to the community as a member of the faculty at the College of Charleston where he also served from time to time as interim president. He would also found a well-regarded school in town called The Athenian Academy.

De Clorivière, called Limöelan by his friends and colleagues, was also an interesting character. Born into a noble family near Nantes in Brittany on November 4, 1768, he was educated at Rennes, the principal city of the province. Among de Clorivière's roommates and close associates at the college in Rennes was the famous French writer François René Chateaubriand and the prominent anti-revolutionist General Jean-Victor Moreau who died fighting with Napoleon in the Russian campaign of 1812. The family de Clorivière were ardent royalists, and his forbears instilled in Limöelan from birth the essential quality of devotion to the king and all the royal institutions of France.

The family was strong in its consistent opposition to the French Revolution and his father was executed by guillotine for supporting the monarchy. After the death of his father, Limöelan joined the Royal Army in support of Louis XVI and Marie Antoinette and participated in the Vendeen Revolt, an important Royalist uprising in western France during the Revolution.

De Clorivière's ardent support of royal institutions was not limited to his anti-revolutionary activities. He opposed any person or institution that planned to replace the king as the sovereign power in France, and he refused to participate in any effort to bring about a reconciliation of the opposing forces after the revolution. The advent of Napoleon Bonaparte as the leader of the nation was anathema to him, and his opposition to the upstart was fierce. He opposed anyone challenging Bourbon royal authority and, as demonstrated by his actions, would use all possible means to prevent the success of anyone he judged to be an enemy of royal authority.

By 1800, Bonaparte had become First Consul of France and was on a path to crown himself as Emperor of the French. De Clorivière boldly decided to try to derail Napoleon's planned progression to power and to open space for the restoration of the nation's monarchy. His plan took the form of a conspiracy to kill Bonaparte. The conspiracy came to be known as the Plot of 3 Nivôse, the revolutionary era date of December 24.

On the assigned day for the execution of the plot, Napoleon and his entourage of two co-conspirators were approaching a theater on rue de la Loi in Paris to see a production of the opera Saul by Haydn. De Clorivière and his fellow conspirators detonated a bomb intended to destroy Napoleon's carriage and its occupants. The powerful explosion occurred near the carriage killing many people close to it, but Napoleon and others in the carriage were miraculously not injured.

One of the three principal conspirators who hatched the plot, Limöelan de Clorivière was the only one of them able to escape with his life. Given a death sentence in absentia for his part in the affair, he escaped detection by hiding in the cellar of the Church of Saint Laurent in Paris. After four months, he was discovered by his uncle and godfather, Pierre-Joseph Picot de Clorivière, a priest who led the restoration of the Jesuits in France after the Revolution and was himself an ardent royalist. His godfather secretly took Limöelan to Brittany and hid him at the estate of his sister, Madame Jean-Baptiste Marc Michel de Chappedelaine.

De Clorivière, recognizing the immediate necessity to leave France, arranged passage on a ship to America. The ship's manifest listed his name as Monsieur Guitry. He was able to get out of France with the aide and assistance of his sister and brother-in-law and his fiancée Julie d'Albert, along with his sister and her family.

It is said that another motivation that led to his departure was the decision made by his fiancée to enter a convent and become a nun in fulfillment of a promise to God for the sparing of his life.

In any case, the three family members left Brittany for America sometime in 1802. Historical records of the period show that his sister, Madame de Chappedelaine, inherited substantial amounts of real estate in the United States including an interest in Sapelo Island near Savannah, Georgia and other lands and attendant assets in New Jersey, Ohio, and Rhode Island.

The de Chappedelaines returned to France after spending a few months in America, leaving de Clorivière to manage their assets and resolve what turned out to be a tangled web of problems concerning the family's property ownership.

His initial base of operations in America was Savannah, Georgia. After several years of wrestling with various disputes around the property ownership and management, including attendance at two sessions of the United States Supreme Court where the de Chappedelaine property interests were at stake, de Clorivière successfully settled most of the land ownership problems.

A lasting influence contributed by de Clorivière was set in place by yet another surprising aspect of his life. It was during the five or so years after his arrival in America that he excelled in painting and selling miniature portraits.

Stephen C. Worsley, writing for the *Journal of Early Southern Decorative Arts*, published an article in 2003 on de Clorivière's contribution to the canon of American miniature portraits, many of which are still exhibited in museums around the country. Some of them can be found in the collection of the Gibbes Art Museum in Charleston. Worsley's presentation in the journal provides many details of the identity of the subjects and where the works are located.

It is interesting that many of the subjects of the miniatures are lawyers he retained to represent him as he sought settlements of the de Chappedelaine family issues, probably executed to defray the costs of the legal services. But his portrait painting career was more than just for settlement of debt. He advertised his availability to paint the miniature portraits in newspapers up and down the east coast of the United States as he traveled on the business of his sister and brother-in-law. Among the known surviving paintings are those of Archbishop John Carroll, Mrs. Nathanael Greene (Catherine Littlefield), and Francis Scott Key.

Limöelan de Clorivière's life took another sharp turn on January 4, 1808, when at age 39 he became a citizen of the United States. Then, on April 9, he entered Saint Mary's Seminary in Baltimore to study for the priesthood. These developments in some ways were not surprising. His interest in the church and the priesthood was apparently influenced by his uncle, who was a prominent cleric in France and the one who helped him most especially by saving his life after the assassination attempt on Napoleon. On the other hand, there was little in Limöelan's life to suggest suitability for or attraction to the priesthood.

Limöelan also knew that Archbishop John Carroll in Baltimore was concerned about the spiritual health of the growing numbers of southern Catholics and recognized the need for more priests in the region.

He completed his course at the seminary and, after his ordination in the spring of 1812, was assigned to assist Father Gallagher in ministering to the many French Catholics, including the royalists who immigrated from Saint Domingue.

De Clorivière served at the Church in Charleston until 1819 but, despite his best efforts, it was a tumultuous time for St. Mary's. The parish leadership, particularly the lay people, long without close episcopal supervision, developed an attitude that it was free of any constraints imposed by anyone and they decided to go their own way in all matters including ecclesiastical ones as only they decided.

The cultural differences in the Irish and the French and smaller numbers of parishioners of other nationalities heightened the conflict and turmoil in the parish. Trustees of the parish, claiming authority to operate as they wished in the face of the authority of the Church hierarchy, kept alive questions of their governing dominance as opposed to the authority of the clergy. Their determination was not softened by the attitudes of Father Gallagher whose own personal characteristics fanned the flames of discord in the parish. He engaged in continuous conflict with Archbishop Carroll mostly springing from his personal habits of intemperance that led to unacceptable conduct. Many complaints were made by parishioners to Archbishop Carroll about all his bad habits including inappropriate language while conducting Mass while in an intoxicated condition. Gallagher became so indignant on one occasion that he went to Rome to personally petition the Pope to be relieved of strictures imposed on him by Carroll. His petition was not granted.

De Clorivière's years in Charleston were full of discord of one sort or another but mostly springing from Gallagher's errant behavior. Gallagher would not allow his fellow priest to assume any authority in the unruly parish—and his allies would not allow de Clorivière to invade his turf. Gallagher thrived amidst the continuous discord. There was a breakdown of order at every level.

Then, when the news was received in Charleston in June 1814 of the abdication of Bonaparte and the restoration of the monarchy in France, de Clorivière ran through the streets of the city singing *a te deum* and shouting *vive le roi* to the great consternation of the inhabitants. (They threatened to shoot him if he didn't quiet down and he finally did.)

This new political scene in France led him to leave for Paris in late 1814, where he was decorated by the new king, Louis XVIII, for his unwavering support of the monarchy during the Revolution and the period of the Empire. He was gone for a year, spending several months in London before returning to Saint Mary's in Charleston in November 1815.

In his absence, conditions at Saint Mary's had not improved. In fact, harmony in the parish had gone steadily downhill in the year he was absent, begging the thought that his personality, which had been blamed for much of the discord, had not been the reason for it. De Clorivière petitioned Archbishop Carroll's successor, Archbishop Neale, also in Baltimore, to allow him to open a chapel in Charleston for the use of French communicants. His request was not granted, but he said Mass on many occasions in houses throughout the city for those who did not wish to tolerate Gallagher's antics.

Relations between Gallagher, some of the Saint Mary's parishioners, and de Clorivière became so strained by early January 1819 that the parish leadership asked Archbishop Marechal, by then Neale's successor, to remove de Clorivière from his position. The Archbishop refused their request, but circumstances were such that de Clorivière could not conduct an effective ministry at any level, so he left Charleston of his own accord.

Lacking local leadership and episcopal direction, Saint Mary's remained in turmoil and discord until the arrival in 1820 of John England as the first bishop of a new diocese embracing the two Carolinas and Georgia.

In 1819, Father de Clorivière became the Director of the Convent of the Visitation at Georgetown, in the District of Columbia, where he served until his death on September 29, 1826. There he supervised the construction and funding for the Church of the Sacred Heart and other buildings on the convent grounds using funds from his estate in Brittany and from his French military pension.

The French king, Charles X, gave him a sculptured scene of Mary and Martha that was used in the façade of the new church building. Revered by the Georgetown community, his body lies in the crypt of the monastery.

ELEVEN
JACQUES CHIRAC'S AMERICAN GIRLFRIEND

Returning from church on a Sunday morning, Colette and Langdon Gibbons stopped by Chapter Two, a local bookstore, to pick up a copy of *The New York Times*. It was a regular habit, as there was no local delivery of *The Times* in those days in Charleston.

The day was unusually cold and rainy for that time of year, so they settled down at home for a lunch of hot soup and nice wine to watch some afternoon television programs. *The Times* was always there on Sunday to inform and entertain them above and beyond the contents of the local paper.

Although she has lived in this country for many years, Colette, a citizen of France, was still not yet a citizen of the U.S. except in spirit. She has a green card that is given to permanent residents, and the government here lists her as a legal alien. Through the years she has retained a fairly strong accent with its various levels, tones, and emphases.

Langdon could often discern something about the nature and complexity and urgency of the issues she raised by the tone of her voice. When she calmly said something like, "Langdon, what do you think about this or that?" he knew it would probably be an easy catch. But when sharply put in a higher than normal tone, he got ready for a tough one.

As they were sitting at home on this particular Sunday, he heard a fastball coming. "Langdon," she said, "do you know someone named Florence Herlihy?"

The question caught him off guard, and he turned toward her to see if he could discern what had led to the question and saw that she was reading *The Times Magazine*. He paused for a few seconds thinking about how to respond to a question about Florence Herlihy.

Thoughts of the old days raced through his mind. After reflecting for a moment, he asked, "Why do you want to know?"

"Because," she said, "Jacques Chirac is looking for her."

"Well, her sister lives on Broad Street, a couple blocks from here."

Florence had been a teenage beauty queen in Orangeburg, a town not far from Charleston where Langdon spent some of his growing-up years. As it was in those days in the Lowcountry, everybody knew everybody, and many of one's friends were related by blood.

Langdon's memory had dimmed about much that had happened in his youth, but he remembered what Florence Herlihy had once looked like in a one-piece white bathing suit on a sunny summer day. She was a little older than Langdon which likely heightened the allure. It was an image that was brilliant and undiminished by the passage of time. He could see Florence in his mind's eye, standing on the grass lawn in the suit, with long flowing hair and very red lipstick. As they say, she was a number.

One of Langdon's classmates in grade school, a neighbor of the Herlihys, confessed that he spent many an hour on summer afternoons trying to catch a glimpse of Florence. Chances are that every red-blooded American boy would have. His friend's advantage was that he lived next door.

"Why in the world is Jacques Chirac looking for Florence?" asked Langdon.

"Because," she said, "they had a love affair up in Boston some years ago, and he hasn't seen her since their parents made them call the thing off, and he can't find her now. So he's looking for her. He wants to see her."

According to the story in *The Times*, Jacques Chirac, the one-time president of France, met Florence in 1953 in Cambridge, Massachusetts. He'd been a student at Harvard for a summer and had had a part-time job as a soda jerk in a Howard Johnson's restaurant. She'd driven up to the restaurant in a white Cadillac convertible with a red top, and had ordered a soda. She'd called him, he said, "Honey Child."

After that, the relationship between the two blossomed. He taught her Latin and she taught him the American way of life. They traveled from the East Coast to the West and back again, enjoying the scenes of the Golden Gate, jazz in New Orleans, and other pleasures in between.

The Times article went on to say that before the summer was over, Jacques had wanted to marry Florence, but when the news reached his parents in France and her parents in South Carolina, the answer had been in the negative.

Was that the end of the story? Langdon wondered.

Maybe. Maybe not. It seemed Chirac had been trying to find Florence for many years, but his efforts had been unsuccessful. He had even asked George H. W. Bush to use the resources of the White House to try to find her. Reportedly, they had tried, but to no avail.

As it happened, Florence's nephew was, like Langdon, a lawyer in town. Intrigued by the mystery, Langdon called him to see if perhaps he would give him her address. The phone rang only once and Langdon posed the simple question. "Paul, where is your Aunt Florence?"

Without a second's delay, the nephew replied, "Why do you want to know? Do you need to sue her?"

Langdon chuckled. "No, Jacques Chirac is looking for her."

The nephew didn't seem to be at all surprised. He happily got the contact information and returned to the phone. "Well, the timing is good. She's not married right now."

Langdon made a copy of *The Times* article and mailed it to a cousin in Paris, along with Florence's then current address and telephone number. The cousin, Jacques de la Ferrièrè, himself a direct descendant of General Thomas Sumter of South Carolina, had recently retired, but had once been a highly-placed diplomat of the government of France and, in more recent times, chief of protocol during the Mitterand administration. Langdon explained the problem to Jacques in the letter, asking him to inform Monsieur le President—through diplomatic channels if necessary—of Florence's whereabouts.

Ambassador de la Ferrièrè responded that he had done what Langdon asked him to do, saying that the information "had been discreetly passed through proper channels to the interested person."

Was that the end of the story?

Maybe, maybe not.

TWELVE
AN AFFAIR OF THE HEART

The events described here did not occur in the Carolina Lowcountry but have strong connections to it. What happened actually took place in France after the French Revolution.

As you know, there are strong historical connections between the French and American Revolutions. Without the French, we might never have succeeded in gaining our independence from England. Then, in 1789, the year the United States Constitution was ratified, France's revolution began, in many ways inspired by what happened here.

The French, determined that Britain should not dominate the North American continent, poured massive monetary, military, and naval support into the American struggle. In fact, the French commitment to the American cause was so substantial that it is believed to have contributed to the demise of France's economy and the government's ability to respond to the needs of its people, leading to the Storming of the Bastille.

You remember that the Marquis de LaFayette was an integral part of our success. Upon his ship's arrival in the colonies, LaFayette went ashore at Prospect Hill, the home of Major Benjamin Huger, and would be taken by Huger to Charleston. He later joined General George Washington and was commissioned a major general in the Continental Army. (It will not be a surprise that Major Huger was an ancestor of our friend Langdon Gibbons.)

One of the tragedies of the French Revolution was the death in prison of the 11-year-old king Louis XVII, son of Louis XVI and Marie Antoinette.

OBITUARY

Paris, June 9, 1795

News has been received of the death yesterday of Louis XVII, king of France and Navarre, at Temple Prison in Paris. Son of the late King Louis XVI and Marie Antoinette, the king was born in the palace at Versailles on March 27, 1785. He is survived by his sister, the Princess Marie Thérèse Charlotte. The king was preceded in death by his parents, by an infant sister, Sophie Hélène Beatrix, and by a brother, le dauphin Louis-Joseph. Funeral arrangements are incomplete because the king's body has disappeared. Arrangements for the funeral will be announced when the king's body is found.

A proper funeral for the boy king was delayed for over two centuries because his body could not be found after his death in the Temple Prison. A surprise announcement was finally made about the funeral in Paris on May 13, 2004.

FUNERAL ARRANGEMENTS FOR LOUIS XVII ARE ANNOUNCED

Paris, May 13, 2004

Plans for the funeral of King Louis XVII of France were announced today in Paris by a spokesperson for Mémorial de France à Saint-Denys. The president of the organizing committee, the Duke of Bauffremont, said the funeral would proceed even though the king's body has not been found. The Duke explained that a recent scientific investigation has confirmed the authenticity of his heart which was removed from his body during an autopsy the day after his death. His heart has been at the Cathedral Basilica of Saint Denis in Paris since 1975 and was previously in the possession of several custodians in France and Italy and across Europe since his death. "The time has arrived", the Duke said, "for the people of France to have a proper funeral for their king."

Along with the notice, the planning committee said a website had been established to provide complete information about the ceremonies, which were set for June 7th and 8th, 2004. An honorary committee of 93 members was formed, headed by Prince Louis de Bourbon, Duke of Anjou, head of the House of Bourbon, and the prospective inheritor of the crown of France.

The committee membership included Austrians with connections to Marie Antoinette, the dead king's mother; members of the House of Bourbon in Italy and in Spain; Yugoslavian and eastern European royals; and many French noblemen. It listed members representing the French Academy; Parisian politicians and various Roman Catholic and other clergy were on the committee, as well as historians and scientists, the Order of Malta, and the American astronaut Buzz Aldrin. The Society of the Cincinnati, a member of which—Prince Louis de Bourbon—was in the line of the dead king's father. And another member of the Society, Langdon Gibbons, was also invited to share in the ceremonies marking the event.

The Society of the Cincinnati was founded in 1783 by General Washington and a few of his fellow officers in the Continental Army, to, among other things, "... render permanent the cordial affection subsisting among the officers." There is a constituent society of The Society of the Cincinnati in each of the states that were the thirteen colonies before independence, and in France.

Washington was elected the first President General of the Society, a position he held until his death. The constituent society in France was also authorized and established by him as Société des Cincinnati de France to recognize the enormous contribution the French army and navy made to the successful conclusion of the American Revolution. Washington personally approved membership applications for the French officers. LaFayette and Rochambeau were original members of the Society in France as well as Langdon's fifth-great-grandfather, Claude François Thomas Marguerite Marie Renart de Fuchsamberg, le marquis d'Amblimont, Brigadier des Armées Navales, who commanded a squadron of French warships that, at the end of the American Revolution, rid the waters off the Massachusetts coast of the remaining British presence.

The Duke announced that ceremonies to lay the king to rest would begin at 10 a.m. on Monday morning, June 7, 2004, when the heart would be viewed by interested onlookers in the church of Saint-Germain-l'Auxerrois, the historic parish church of the royal family adjacent to the Louvre, which was itself a former royal palace.

All the events around the funeral would be conducted in the presence of Prince Louis de Bourbon. There would be a Requiem Mass offered for the repose of the king's soul in Saint-Germain-l'Auxerrois on Monday evening at 6 p.m., followed by a small dinner at the Jockey Club of Paris.

The announcement continued:

> The ceremonies on Tuesday, June 8, the anniversary of the king's death, will begin at 10 am at the Cathedral Basilica of Saint Denis where Jean Cardinal Honoré, a sometime archbishop of Tours, will preside at a Solemn Mass honoring the Sacred Heart. The Mass will be conducted in the presence of Monseigneur Fofiunato Baldelli, the Apostolic Delegate to France, and Prince Louis de Bourbon. Those attending the ceremonies are invited to a luncheon at the conclusion of the Mass in the Legion of Honor School that is adjacent to the Basilica. At 3 pm, people attending the luncheon are invited to return to the Basilica for the interment of the king's heart in the crypt where the remains of his parents, Marie Antoinette and Louis XVI, are interred near many of the other French monarchs.

It was a signal honor for Langdon to be invited to attend the funeral of the late king's heart and to participate in the activities in connection with it. He and Colette were extraordinarily honored, as a part of the small contingency of American members of the Society of Cincinnati and were asked to sit immediately behind the family of the late king in the Basilica of Saint Denis.

The Backstory

Born Louis-Charles in the palace at Versailles on March 27, 1785, the future king became the dauphin on June 4, 1789, upon the death of Louis Joseph, his older brother. The growing intensity of the French Revolution led to the imprisonment of the royal family in August 1792 in the Temple Prison, a dark and dank tower on the grounds of the former palace of the Count d'Artois.

The king and queen would never again breathe the air of freedom. Louis XVI was executed on January 27, 1793, and his wife, Marie Antoinette, met the same fate ten months later. The revolutionaries separated the new king Louis XVII from his mother four months before her death. By all accounts, the boy was treated inhumanely by the guards until he died from a combination of consumption (tuberculosis) and maltreatment two years later, on June 8, 1795. Some of the accounts of his life in prison reveal that he was tortured and tormented, forced to curse the memory of his mother and to sing revolutionary songs.

The day after the boy king's death, a Paris physician, Philippe-Jean Pelletan, performed an autopsy on the body. The doctor reportedly removed the heart and took it home with him where he kept in a desk drawer.

The heart remained, more or less, in the custody of the Pelletan family until 1895, with two exceptions. It was stolen in 1810 by Jean-Henri Tillos, the doctor's assistant.

Tillos confessed the theft to members of his family while on his deathbed, and they returned the heart to Pelletan. On another occasion, in the late 1820s, Pelletan gave the heart to the Archbishop of Paris for safekeeping. It was lost in the disorder caused by the Revolution of 1830 when the young king's uncle, Charles X, was dethroned. The Archbishop's palace was ransacked, the crystal urn containing the heart was shattered, and the heart lost. Pelletan's son, Philippe-Gabriel Pelletan, miraculously found it in a trash pile near the Archbishop's palace and once again restored it to the Pelletan family home.

One hundred years after the young king's death, his heart was finally restored to the House of Bourbon—the dead king's family— when Édouard Dumont, a relative of the wife of Philippe-Henri Pelletan, presented it to Don Carlos de Bourbon, Duke of Madrid, then the Bourbon heir to the throne of France.

Spanish Bourbons gained the right of inheritance to the French crown when the last of the male line descending from Charles X died in 1883. Under the prevailing principles of Salic Law, the historic rules that are used to settle questions of royal inheritance, the right to the crown of France was acquired by descendants of Felipe V, the king of Spain who was a grandson of Louis XIV.

Don Carlos took the heart of the boy king to the chapel of the Château de Frohsdorf in Austria, which had been the home of Marie-Thérèse, the Duchess of Angoulême, the young king's sister and the only family survivor of the imprisonment. She had lived there with her husband after release from the Temple Prison. The heart remained there but was almost lost again when, in 1942, the Nazi army occupied the chateau.

By some miracle, it was again rescued and taken to Italy by Princess Massimo, the daughter of Don Carlos, where it was kept by members of the Italian branch of the House of Bourbon. It remained in Italy until 1975, when a daughter of the Italian princess gave the heart to the Duke de Bauffremont, president of Mémorial de France à Saint-Denys, who stored it in the crypt at the Basilica of Saint-Denis in Paris.

As revealed in the obituary, the funeral for the king could not be planned until it was established that the body was indeed lost and that the heart now at the Basilica was all of it that remained anywhere.

There was plenty of uncertainty about what had happened to the king's body if, in fact, he had really died. After his death was reported, persistent rumors spread all over Europe and elsewhere that royalist sympathizers had aided his escape, and that another boy's body had been left as a decoy. These rumors led many to believe that the heart in the Basilica at Saint-Denis was, after all, not the heart of the king at all.

As a result, there were contemporary claims by some to be the dauphin who had escaped from the prison. Descendants of some of the claimants in later generations said they were entitled to the throne of France as his direct descendants.

Another enduring claim to the throne that continues to this day is that of Karl Wilhelm Naundorff, a Prussian clockmaker, and his descendants. He, in 1831, announced that he was *le dauphin* and that he had escaped from the Temple Prison in June 1795. Upon the urging of family and friends, Naundorff went to Paris to mount a campaign for recognition as Louis XVII. He ingratiated himself to former members of the royal household and was able to convince some of them that he was the king.

His eccentric conduct intensified over the years as he bestowed many royal titles on followers. Naundorff was imprisoned for debt in England in the early 1840s and died in Holland in 1845. His death certificate and tombstone identify him as King Louis XVII of France.

The efforts of the Naundorff family for recognition did not end with Karl Wilhelm's death, however. His descendants continue the effort to establish themselves as the inheritors of the Bourbon crown. So far, they have failed.

Naundorff was not the only pretender to the throne. There have been over 40 claimants in all, and there have been many more rumors of a living Bourbon king in France and throughout the western world. One that persisted in the United States well into the twentieth century was that John James Audubon, the naturalist and painter, was the boy king. Following his escape from prison, he had settled in America.

Finally, in the 1990s, reliable scientific evidence emerged that finally made it possible to conclude with certainty that the heart in the crystal urn at the Basilica was indeed that of Louis XVII. A French historian, Philippe Delorme, in concert with the Duke of Bauffremont, arranged DNA testing to determine if there was any validity to the claims to inheritance the Naundorff family. The Belgian scientist, Jean-Jacques Cassiman, gathered samples from Naundorff's descendants and from the hair of Marie Antoinette for a comparative analysis.

The test was conducted and Cassiman's report was published in the *European Journal of Human Genetics* in 1998. "… "it becomes very unlikely that Karl Wilhelm Naundorff is the son of Marie Antoinette," wrote Cassiman, ruling the Naundorff family was unrelated to the House of Bourbon and had no claim to the throne of France.

In December 1999, it was decided to apply the same scientific techniques to determine if the heart in the crystal urn at Saint-Denis was, in fact, from the body of Louis XVII.

There were not enough DNA samples remaining from the hair of Marie Antoinette after the Naundorff test, so a search was undertaken for DNA samples from other members of the family. A rosary that had belonged to Marie-Thérèsa, mother of Marie Antoinette, was found in the Elizabethan convent in Klagenfurt, Austria. Its beads contained strands of the hair of her children.

The heart was ceremoniously taken by hearse to a laboratory in Paris where small pieces of tissue were extracted. Painstaking care was taken to ensure the integrity of the test procedures—all scientists used recognized scientific standards to guarantee proper custody, care, control, and testing of the samples. A DNA sample from each of the sources was given to Professor Cassiman, and also to Professor Bernard Brinkman for testing at Münster University in Germany.

Both Cassiman and Brinkman reported matches of the samples they tested—the DNA of the heart tissues and that of the hair from the rosary included identical strands. The two scientists held a press conference in Paris on April 19, 2000 to announce the results. Cassiman and Brinkman were joined by the historian, Philippe Delorme, and the Duke of Bauffremont. The announcement was also attended by Prince Louis de Bourbon, Duke of Anjou, and the head of the House of Bourbon, as well as by members of the Naundorff family. Cassiman said, "The comparison of the DNA appeared to show beyond all reasonable doubt that the heart came from a child that was maternally related to the Hapsburg family ... all this taken with the historical record, provides strong evidence to support the proposition that this is the heart of the lost dauphin."

Thus, with all obstacles removed 205 years after the king's death, plans for the funeral could finally proceed—with the heart.

Saint Germain l'Auxerrois is the historic church of the French royal families. It is across the street from the eastern end of the Louvre, the old palace of French kings and now perhaps the most famous museum of art in the world.

The gothic church's origins reach back to the 12th century, and its elegant stained glass dates to the 15th. On June 7, 2004, it was the scene of a requiem mass for the repose of the soul of a king of France on the eve of the 209th anniversary of his death.

The Mass began at 6 pm. The church was packed with people—sitting, standing, and kneeling in every nook and cranny. An overflow crowd stood on the portico in front of the church and in the street.

Langdon and Colette stood for the Mass next to a gothic column in the church about 10 or 12 feet from the altar as there was not a vacant seat anywhere. There were men and women, young and old, nuns, priests, noblemen, and crowds of ordinary people. Many news reporters with cameras had stationed themselves in the front of the church near the altar to record the scene. The clergy conducting the mass were dressed in black chasubles appropriate for the occasion.

After the Mass began, the congregation suddenly and spontaneously erupted in applause and shouting as the presiding priest was about halfway through the introductory prayer. The cause of the eruption was the arrival of Prince Louis de Bourbon. The congregation soon respectfully settled, and the Mass continued in due course and form to the end.

When it ended about 7:30 p.m., the crowd left the church. Some of them drifted toward the Jockey Club for a dinner sponsored by the Mémorial de France à Saint-Denys. There were about 70 people at the dinner including Prince Louis, the Duke of Bauffremont, members of the organizing committee, members of The Society of the Cincinnati—including Langdon and Colette—and a few others involved in the funeral events.

The mood was both festive and somber. It was a sad occasion, as funeral events usually are, but festive because it was finally happening after centuries of waiting as the human remains of a king of France were about to finally be laid to rest. It was a family affair, honoring the past and looking toward the future.

It was also a happy occasion because it brought to an end a long quest for official recognition of the truth about the origin of the king's heart that would be laid next to his parents. It marked the end of any real doubt about the legitimacy of the claim of the House of Bourbon to the throne should France ever decide to again establish a monarchy.

The Cathedral Basilica of Saint-Denis is built on the place where Saint Denis, the first bishop of Paris and patron saint of France, is said to have died in 250 A.D. Legend has it that Denis, a native of Greece, was beheaded near Montmartre for denying the divinity of the Roman emperor. The story about his death is that he walked 6,000 paces with his head in his hand until he fell. The Basilica was built on the spot.

It is the first known church to be built in gothic style, and was completed in its present form in the 13th century. The crypt beneath the altar is the resting place for most of the kings and queens of France. Bodies of 42 kings and 32 queens are interred there, including Charles Martel, Pepin the Short, and Charlemagne, the great first Holy Roman Emperor, who was crowned on Christmas Day in 800 AD. Hugh, the first king of the Capetian dynasty and a descendant of Charlemagne, is also there with most of his successors, including Louis XVI and Marie Antoinette, and after two centuries, their child Louis XVII.

The Basilica is tucked into the crowded narrow streets of the village of Saint-Denis on the northern side of Paris, just outside the beltway that circles the city. One approaches the dark stone edifice from the rue de Strasbourg across a courtyard of smooth paving stones about 75 yards from the street. The church building, still in classic gothic style, is beautiful—with light filtering into it through magnificent stained glass windows.

The altar used for the Mass is situated, in modern style, in the chancel, conforming to the liturgical reforms of the Second Vatican Council. Cathedral or chapel-style chairs, estimated at more than a thousand, were placed throughout the nave and the transepts for the seating of the congregation at the funeral.

The Solemn Mass of the Sacred Heart was scheduled to begin at 10 am, and people who had been invited to attend the ceremonies began taking their seats at 9 a.m. There were throngs of onlookers in the streets as people began to arrive at the doors of the Basilica. Admission to the Mass was tightly controlled, and the cathedral doors were guarded to prevent the entrance of anyone without proper documentation. No cameras or other recording devices were allowed.

A symphonic orchestra occupied a platform just inside the entrance doors of the church. Soon after 9 a.m., the orchestra began playing fanfares that were suitable for royal settings by Jean-Baptiste Pergolèse, George Frederick Handel, and other musical selections appropriate for the burial of a king. Music for the Mass was sung by the Gregorian Choir of Paris.

A pedestal, about six feet high, occupied a place to the left of the altar and was draped with a green cloth emblazoned with gold fleur-de-lis, the royal symbol of France. The crown of France and Navarre was placed atop the pedestal and on a shelf below it, the crystal urn containing the king's heart would rest.

The first 15 or 20 rows of chairs in the nave of the church were reserved for the family of the deceased king—occupied by members of the House of Bourbon in France, Spain, and Italy. Behind the family were seated the members of The Society of the Cincinnati.

Prince Louis de Bourbon was seated in the first row of chairs on the right side of the church, and at 10 a.m. sharp, wafts of incense began to float across the nave, signaling the procession of clergy and other participants in the Mass. The urn containing the heart of the king was carried in the procession by a young boy who was a member of the Italian House of Bourbon de Parme. As he approached the chancel steps, a member of the clergy took the urn from him and placed it below the crown. The Mass was celebrated according to the Roman rite, and the homily was presented by the presiding cleric, Jean Cardinal Honoré of Tours.

When the Mass ended at a little before 1 p.m., the congregation walked out of the church through the door at the western transept, across a narrow yard, and into the Girl's School of the Legion of

Honor. The school building there is square and covers an area about the size of a city block. There is an enclosed cloister on the inside perimeter of the school building surrounding a large garden in the center.

Tables for ten people each were set up all around the cloister, providing luncheon place settings for everyone who had attended the ceremonies in the church. At the beginning of the luncheon, during many sociable exchanges among the guests at the nearby tables, Langdon saw a familiar looking face across the table from him. Unable to put a name to the face, he introduced himself.

"Hello, I'm Langdon Gibbons from Charleston."

"Glad to meet you," said the man. "I'm Buzz Aldrin."

After a lunch with champagne, wine, and several courses, the congregants were asked to return to their same seats for the service of the interment of the heart.

The last part of the journey of the heart began with scripture readings and prayers in the sanctuary of the Basilica.

When the prayers ended, Prince Louis de Bourbon arose from his seat in the front of the nave and walked up the steps to the pedestal next to the altar. He removed the crystal urn containing the heart and followed a procession of clergy to the left of the altar, down a winding staircase into the Bourbon Chapel of the crypt.

A niche had been cut into the base of a monument that had been erected in honor of the young king by Louis XVIII, his uncle and his successor on the throne. Prince Louis de Bourbon gently placed the urn with the heart in the niche, near the remains of his parents, whose slabs were covered with large bouquets of white lilies. And so it was that King Louis XVII was finally laid to rest.

What is the meaning of it all? Edith Wharton, the American writer who lived in France and wrote about its national life in the early twentieth century, said that the measure of a nation's civilization is in how she tends her flower garden. She defined the national flower garden as the place where the arts and graces flourish to support all that is important.

The burial of the heart of Louis XVII and the grace that flowed from the momentous events of June 7 and 8, 2004 sprang forcefully from France's highly cultivated national flower garden. The funeral for young Louis brought back memories of a time in France that was filled with turmoil, terror, and death in the midst of the bloodiest revolution in western history, but it also closed a chapter of that history that had lingered as an open sore for two centuries.

Just as a chapter of history was closed, another was opened by these events. The new chapter looks to the future. It opened a path for those in the enthusiastic crowds surrounding the events of the funeral who think there should be a king in France. For them, all the elements for a French monarchy are now in place. Modern science has established that Prince Louis de Bourbon, the Duke of Anjou, is the rightful heir of Louis XVII, and that if France ever decides that it wishes to institute another Bourbon monarchy in succession to the old one, he and his successors are there and ready to accept the responsibilities given to them.

Although the king's heart now lies at rest, there is one affair of the heart that will never end — the bond of loyalty and honor that bridges an ocean, begun between George Washington and the Marquis de LaFayette. It will forever connect the lives of those on both sides who would change the world.

ACKNOWLEDGMENTS

The history of the South Carolina Lowcountry that is portrayed in this book is based in large part upon the contributions of Walter B. Edgar to the understanding of our history. He is a valued friend and colleague in many common endeavors. His *South Carolina, A History* (University of South Carolina Press, 1998) has been an invaluable and most credible resource for the exposition of the history of the Lowcountry from its genesis to this day. Everyone who is interested in learning about our past to help guide us into the future will benefit from his valuable work. We are all indebted to him.

Perhaps the greatest yet unfathomed element in the search for understanding the historic culture of the South Carolina Lowcountry is the institution of slavery. It was introduced in the Carolina Colony at the same time the first permanent European colonists arrived in 1670. Our understanding of how it developed over time in the early colonial days is masterfully set out in *Atlas Of The Transatlantic Slave Trade* by David Eltis and David Richardson (Yale University Press, 2010). It is upon the information provided by this valuable work that I was able to write a historical background leading to the essays in this work based on the lives of people emerging from slavery. Those who recognize the importance of understanding the institution of slavery are indebted to these scholars for their contribution to the search.

The people, the real human beings, whose lives are portrayed in the essays following the historical backgrounds of the English, African, and French immigration deserve all the substantive credit for helping us understand what life has been like in the Carolina Lowcountry from the beginning of its colonization by Europeans and Africans. The history tells us how they got here, the essays seek to uncover what it was really like.

I most especially thank a valued colleague, Elizabeth W. Hodges, for her contributions to this work by editing, researching, formatting the presentation, and persistent strong support and encouragement to bring this work to fruition.

Finally, I am most grateful to Gaya Mitra for consenting to the use of one of her magnificent photographs for the cover of this book. It portrays all the important elements of what this book is about: sunrise, clouds, land, and people.

ABOUT THE AUTHOR

THOMAS TISDALE is a lawyer and writer living in Charleston, South Carolina. A former president of the South Carolina Historical Society and the South Carolina Bar, he has served on the boards of several schools and colleges and community-related non-profit organizations, including the University of the South and Spoleto Festival, USA. Tisdale is the author of the biography *A Lady of the High Hills: Natalie Delage Sumter* (University of South Carolina Press, 2001). In 2004, he was the executive producer of the play *South* by Julian Green and in 2013, wrote a play *Truth in Cold Blood*.

He was a founder of SPCK/USA, the American branch of the oldest English missionary society that distributes Christian literature worldwide.

CPSIA information can be obtained
at www.ICGtesting.com
Printed in the USA
FFOW04n1252030117
30969FF